*To all those who have helped in any way
in the preservation, conservation and consolidation
of the Roman Wall*

Memory and history both derive and gain emphasis from physical remains. Tangible survivals provide a vivid immediacy that helps to assure us there really was a past. Physical remains have their limitations as informants, to be sure: they are themselves mute, requiring interpretation; their continual but differential erosion and demolition skews the record; and their substantial survival conjures up a past more static than could have been the case. But however depleted by time and use, relics remain essential bridges between then and now. They confirm or deny what we think of it, symbolize or memorialize communal links over time, and provide archaeological metaphors that illumine the processes of history and memory.

David Lowenthal, *The Past is a Foreign Country* (1985)

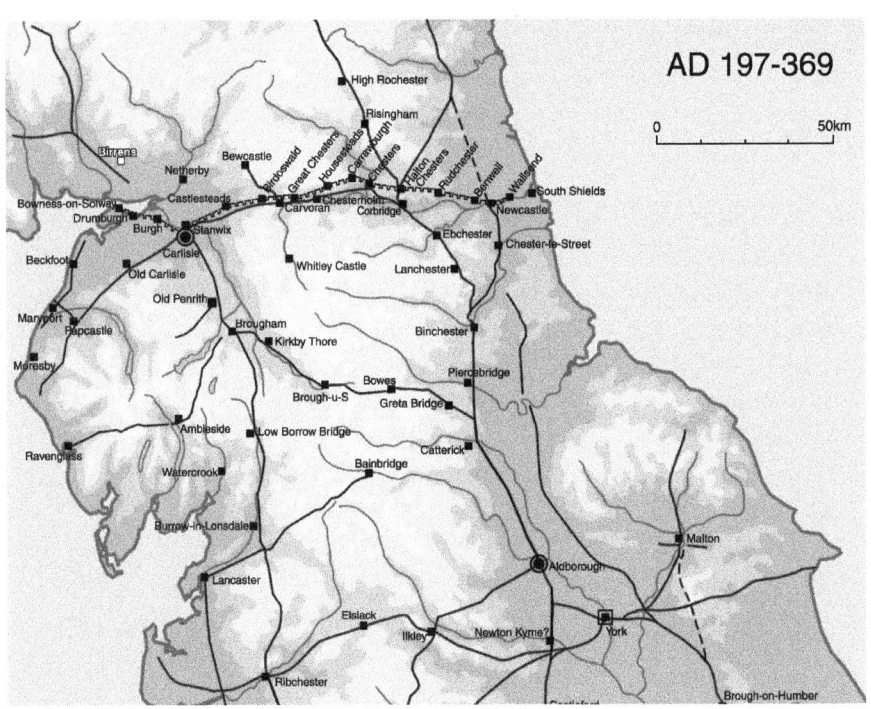

Hadrian's Wall. (© TWM Archaeology)

SAVING THE WALL

THE CONSERVATION OF HADRIAN'S WALL
1746 – 1987

STEPHEN LEACH & ALAN WHITWORTH

AMBERLEY

First published 2011

Amberley Publishing
The Hill, Stroud
Gloucestershire, GL5 4EP

www.amberleybooks.com

British Library Cataloguing in Publication Data.
A catalogue record for this book is available from the British Library.

ISBN 978-1-4456-0018-5

Typeset in 10pt on 12pt Sabon.
Typesetting and Origination by Amberley Publishing.
Printed in the UK.

Contents

Acknowledgements

First of all we would like to thank Mr Charles Anderson's daughter, Mrs A. Luscombe, for permission to use her late father's notes and photographs, and other relevant material. Thanks to Andrew Poad; and Kirsten Jarrett for help integrating the photographs into the text; and to Georgina Plowright and David Breeze for the Clayton family tree. Thanks to Robin and Anthony Birley for permission to reproduce those of their father's poems that concern the conservation of the Wall. And, finally, our thanks also go to Paul Bidwell for having proofread the entire document and for his general guidance. Those errors and shortfalls that remain are of course the responsibility of the authors alone.

Abbreviations

Figures

Part I

Conservation

Prologue

The story of how Hadrian's Wall was saved is also the story of how it was almost lost. This book attempts to tell that story in as much detail as its authors were able to include without losing sight of the central plot. However, before delving into the details of the story, it may be useful to sketch that story here, in its broadest outline.

The story begins with the construction of General Wade's Military Road (beginning in 1746). The Military Way runs in part under the present B6318 and was built in the wake of Jacobite Rebellion, with the aim of enabling the rapid movement of troops from Newcastle to Dumfriesshire. Stone from the Wall was extensively reused in its foundations and, indeed, this is without doubt the single most destructive event in the Wall's history. The antiquarian William Stukeley called for legislation to prevent its destruction: 'Is it not to be regretted, in an age of Building and Architecture, that this British boast and glory should be destroyed?' (Piggott 1985, 145–46) But his protest went unheeded. Yet, though ineffective, Stukeley's protest was the harbinger of others that were more successful. Possibly the echo of Stukeley's protest acted as a brake upon the destruction of the Wall in subsequent years, although this is of course difficult to demonstrate.

The appeal of the Wall stones, for reuse as road foundations or for farm buildings, remained. Thus when William Hutton, of Birmingham, walked the length of the wall in July 1801, at the age of seventy-eight, he found a portion of the Wall being demolished (at Planetrees in the vicinity of turret 25b) (Hutton 1802). The proprietor of that portion of land, Henry Tulip, had already removed 95 yards of stonework in order to build a farmhouse. In his *History of the Wall*, Hutton laments that he had not set off sooner – for what then might he have seen! However, according to local tradition, although the act of demolition had already begun, it was owing to Hutton's tears and entreaties that the proprietor refrained from razing the Wall completely.

Following Hutton's timely intervention, the first systematic conservation of the Wall began with the purchases of John Clayton (1792–1890). In the 1830s

John Clayton, whose family owned the fort of Chesters (Cilurnum), had been concerned by the sight of parts of the Wall being carried away in contractors' carts to build houses. With the aim of preventing the recurrence of such incidents, he began to purchase farmland in the central sector of the Wall, including the fort at Housesteads (Vercovicium) in 1838. Probably influenced by the Reverend John Hodgson (who had begun opening up parts of the monument in the early nineteenth century), Clayton also began to open up sections of the monument and to carry out excavations – his main campaigns probably taking place between 1848 and 1873. Lengths of so-called 'Clayton Wall' can be seen to this day at Peel Crags, Hotbank Crags and Cuddy's Crag, within the National Trust Estate. Clayton's ambition was not only to protect the Wall from those in search of stone, but also 'to secure the landscape setting of the Wall and its forts' (Crow 2004, 133). In his attention to the land surrounding the Wall, Clayton probably did not trouble to distinguish between aesthetic motives and archaeological: both demanded that the Wall should be seen – so far as possible – as the Romans had last seen it.

Clayton's policies worked well. He allowed public access and he prevented the robbing of stone, but his powers were confined to his own estate. Beyond his estate, from the late nineteenth century a threat was posed not only by farmers in search of building stone, but also by quarries. Thus, when the Walltown Turret (45b) was discovered in 1883, it was threatened from the outset by quarrying. Its destruction was predicted by Collingwood Bruce in 1883 (Collingwood Bruce 1883, 235) and soon afterwards his worst fears were realised.

But however extensive Clayton's estate became, the Wall was ultimately dependent upon its owner's interest and financial security. When John Maurice ('Jack') Clayton inherited the estate and shortly afterwards fell into debt, the outlook for the Wall seemed bleak indeed, for at the same time a new quarry threatened the previously protected central section of the Wall. (Ironically, it was the increasing number of cars on the roads, including those of day-trippers on their way to Hadrian's Wall, that had led to the demand for their improvement – thereby increasing the orders for stone from the very quarries that threatened the Wall.)

The Wall's owners were not allowed to alter it in any way without permission from the government – but as archaeologists had long realised, the danger posed by an expanding quarry was not necessarily that of *direct* destruction, for if a quarry advanced close enough to the Wall a sector might easily disappear in a landslip. Also, the Wall would be left in an almost entirely different situation within the landscape than it had formerly been.

In the face of this threat, archaeologists felt impelled to take action and to call upon all the resources at their disposal. They realised that their major asset was the warmth of public opinion. Archaeologists were able to reap the benefits of a public interest in archaeology that had grown steadily since the turn of the century, stimulated, in the case of Hadrian's Wall, by the benevolence of the Clayton estate and by such books as Kipling's *Puck of Pook's Hill*, and by Collingwood's guides listing accommodation near to the Wall.

Archaeologists determined to make the best use possible of the weight of public opinion, so that not only would the immediate threat to the Wall be repulsed, but it might also be eradicated for the foreseeable future. (In virtue of this ambition, the archaeologists of this period might be termed not only conservationists but also custodians.) The result was the 1931 Ancient Monuments Act, granting the First Commissioner of HM Works the power to make planning schemes and to pay compensation to those affected. However, there was a series of delays before the act was implemented. When it was eventually enforced, the Act protected the surroundings of the central section of the Wall by means of the Wall and Vallum Preservation Scheme. The latter part of this episode was described by the late John Charlton in an article entitled 'Saving the Wall'. Being unable to better this title, and in respect for John Charlton's memory, the authors adopted it for the present volume.

Before its official ratification in 1943, the Wall and Vallum Preservation Scheme was implemented informally; and after its ratification it continued in existence until its absorption into the Northumberland National Park in 1956. That the southern boundary of the National Park should today coincide for much of its length with the former boundary of the Preservation Scheme is quite fitting; for in many ways the Roman Wall and Vallum Preservation Scheme can be seen as a forerunner to Britain's National Parks. Indeed the story of the Roman Wall and Vallum Preservation Scheme, and of Clayton's estate, belongs in many respects to the first chapter of a history of Britain's National Parks.

After the passing of the Ancient Monuments Act and the unofficial implementation of the Preservation Scheme, there were donations of sections of the Wall to the National Trust and directly to the state, encouraged both by public spirit and perhaps a wish to avoid death duties.

These donations enabled the exposure and consolidation of the Wall to continue apace; and this is the main subject of the second part of the book. It is not generally realised that prior to 1931 the main sections of the Wall 'open to view' were those that had been opened up by Clayton at Housesteads Crags, Peel Crags and Steel Rigg. The Wall at Birdoswald, Willowford, Walltown, Cawfields, Winshields, Peel Crag, Sycamore Gap and Mons Fabricius was still covered with soil, trees and fences.

In general we have tried to confine the term 'preservation' to the defence from direct harm of the Wall itself, such as when Hutton persuaded the farmer to stop dismantling it. The term 'conservation' is used to refer to practices intended to preserve the Wall through the care of its surroundings; and the term 'consolidation' is used to refer to practices intended to preserve the Wall through the care of the Wall's fabric. All three sets of practices are of course inextricably linked – just as in any military campaign, one set of practices, from communications to cooking, is reliant upon another – but at different times focus has shifted from one to the other.

Consolidation is perhaps the least dramatic of these practices and also perhaps the least understood by the general public. The methods of consolidation have, as will be seen, occasionally generated controversy, in that the consolidation of the Wall as an aesthetic object in the landscape has been seen to conflict with the consolidation of the Wall as a source of historical information. This controversy reached its height in the wake of Jacquetta Hawkes' articles in the *Observer* in 1958. However, since then beauty and science seem to have settled some of their differences, and it is recognised that while those sectors that remain unexposed and unconsolidated may be less aesthetically attractive, and attract fewer visitors, they remain potentially the most valuable sectors to the archaeologists of the future. In particular, there are long stretches of the Wall in the east and west that remain unexposed, and unmentioned in this book: it should not be inferred that these stretches are of any less archaeological interest than the better-known central sectors. (Nor should it be inferred that survival in these sectors is entirely owing to chance.)

Yet for all the changes of emphasis in this story, there is also an essential continuity of purpose. The designation of the Wall as a World Heritage Site in 1987 is surely an act that Clayton himself would have appreciated.

The Turn of a Card

The Clayton estate continued to successfully maintain and protect substantial sections of the Wall until 1929. The estate appointed F. G. Simpson as a sort of archaeological land agent and Mr Thomas Thompson as guide and caretaker at Housesteads. It was John Clayton's nephew, Nathaniel George, who conceived the idea of the Chesters museum. The present museum was built in 1903, though a collection of artefacts was on display from 1896.

However, beyond the Clayton estate, a threat was posed by quarries at Cawfields and Walltown. At the turn of the century, the quarry at Walltown destroyed a section of the Wall near the fort of Carvoran; and at some point after its opening in 1902 the quarry at Cawfields destroyed a section of the Wall between Burnhead Cottage and Hole Gap just west of milecastle 42 (Woodside and Crow 1999, 92). A photograph in F. G. Simpson's *Watermills and Military Works on Hadrian's Wall: Excavations in Northumberland 1907-13*, reproduced below, records the ruins of a building beside this stretch of the Wall, on Burnhead Crag, that was destroyed at this time – the date of these remains is now, in retrospect, all but impossible to determine.

In 1929, in his *Guide to the Wall*, R. G. Collingwood warned that 'Cawfields Quarry is steadily consuming the Whin Sill, and the Wall with it.' (Collingwood 1929, 27). However, it was the central section the Wall that would soon face an even greater threat.

The Wall that lay within the boundaries of the 20,000-acre Clayton estate – including the five Wall forts, Housesteads (Vercovicium), Carrawbrugh (Procolita), Carvoran (Magna), Chesterholm (Vindolanda) and Chesters (Cilurnum) – was thought to be safeguarded. But for how long? When Mrs Isabel Clayton died in April 1928 and the estate was inherited by John Maurice ('Jack') Clayton, the grandson of Nathaniel George, it was thought only prudent that the Wall should join the list of scheduled monuments. It was scheduled on 18 December 1928. One wonders if there was a presentiment of danger even at this date.

As it was, the fate of the Wall turned on the fall of a card – or the fall of a dice – at White's in Piccadilly. (Horse racing was also involved in some versions of the story.) The estate was put up for sale just over a year after Mrs Clayton's death, in order to pay Jack Clayton's gambling debts.

Saving the Wall

1.1. The Building on Burnhead Crag. (F. G. Simpson)

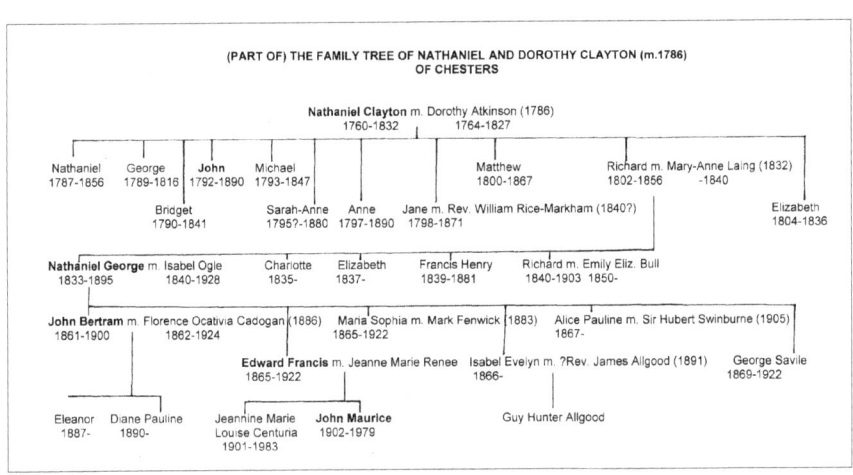

1.2. The Clayton family tree.

The estate was divided into lots to be auctioned in a great two-day sale on 19 and 20 July 1929 at the Old Assembly Rooms in Newcastle. Fortunately, the young archaeologist Eric Birley, who was excavating milecastle 9 at the time, heard of the sale and was determined to place a bid. His initial idea was to bid for Carrawburgh,

> but he accepted the advice of his senior excavator, Thomas Hepple, the excavator of the Vindolanda well for the Clayton estate in 1914, who advised him that the Vindolanda remains were far better preserved. (Birley 2009, 26)

So, with his father's financial backing, he bought Vindolanda.

> For the record, the day after the Clayton sale the agent came to see him, to report that the neighbouring property of Housesteads had failed to attract a buyer. 'Would Mr. Birley like to purchase that as well?' Sadly, his funds did not stretch that far. (Birley 2009, 26)

A short while later, the fort at Housesteads and a length of Wall – up to and including milecastle 37 to the west and Knag Burn Gateway to the east – was given to the National Trust. *The Times* praised Jack Clayton for his generosity (31 January 1930) but, behind the scenes, it seems likely that the vice-chairman of the National Trust, the historian Professor George Trevelyan of Wallington Hall in Northumberland, may have had a hand in persuading Jack Clayton to make this donation, for a letter from George Trevelyan to Jack Clayton dated 10 September 1929, on exhibition at Wallington Hall in August 2009, insists that the camp and the farm are dealt with together. It seems likely that Trevelyan agreed to buy Housesteads Farm only on condition that the fort of Housesteads be given to the National Trust or the Office of Works. Subsequently, George Trevelyan acquired the remainder of Housesteads Farm (320 acres), and eventually it too was passed on to the Trust (Crow 2004, 135). These, in brief, were the circumstances by which the National Trust began to acquire a substantial landholding in the central section of the Wall.

Thus 1930 began optimistically with Vindolanda and Housesteads (Vercovicium) in safekeeping – but any optimism as regards the Wall's safety was soon to be dashed.

A Knife's Edge

On 11 April 1930, *The Times* broke the news of imminent danger in the following strident announcement:

Hadrian's Wall, which in ancient days withstood the inroads of barbarism and for centuries has offered a stout resistance to time and weather, is now threatened with violence in a new form. It is proposed to carry out extensive quarrying operations in the soil on which it stands. A company is, it is understood, formed for this purpose, and work over a very large area is proposed. While a threat to such a monument as Hadrian's Wall is a matter for national rather than local concern, the first protest that it has provoked comes suitably enough from the Society of Antiquaries of Newcastle-upon-Tyne.

In the words of the Newcastle Antiquaries, quoted by *The Times* verbatim:

[In] the neighbourhood of Shields-on-the-Wall, Pele Crag [*sic*], and Housesteads, in Northumberland, including five miles of the finest stretch of the Wall, and also of the most characteristic Wall scenery ... [much] of the Wall is already destroyed, but this section includes the finest remaining stretch. This and the wild country to the north of it should be acquired by the State and maintained by HM Office of Works, and the amenities of the district might be preserved by making it a national park. Although the Wall is scheduled as an ancient monument, it appears that the present Ancient Monuments Protection Acts are insufficient to protect it from such an attack. If so, the State should take legislative action ...

Leaving its readers in no doubt as to the gravity of the situation, *The Times* then went on to remark that

if the project were pushed to its natural conclusion a long stretch of the most beautiful and characteristic scenery through which the Wall and Vallum run, together with the fort at Housesteads, the Borcovicus of Roman times, lately presented by Mr. J.M. Clayton to the National Trust, would be threatened with oblivion. The slopes leading up to the Wall would be marked by quarries, while the Wall itself, as the resolution shows, would be left on the summit of steep cliffs, a meaningless object, inaccessible from the south, and having no relation to the formation of the country which influenced those who chose the site on which it was built.

Ancient monuments were at this time protected by two Acts of Parliament: the Ancient Monuments Protection Act (1882) and the Ancient Monument Consolidation and Amendment Act (1913). The 1882 Act required that if the owner of an ancient monument wished to destroy it, he should first give the nation the option of purchasing it. To this end, it was the job of an Inspector of Ancient Monuments to negotiate with the owners on behalf of the government. The 1913 Act made provisions for the commissioners of works of the Ancient Monuments Boards of England, Scotland and Wales (consisting of archaeologists, historians and representatives of learned societies and interested public bodies) to advise the Ministry of Works on placing preservation orders on monuments in imminent danger of destruction or damage. The boards had the power to inspect any monuments facing such danger, even against the wishes of their owners. Furthermore, Historic Buildings Councils were set up to provide advice to the Ministry of Works on the acquisition of ancient monuments and on the assistance that should be given to the National Trust to acquire buildings of historical interest. Curiously, during the nineteenth century most of the monuments that were scheduled were of the prehistoric period and, in general, Roman monuments were not scheduled until after 1920. 'Prior to 1920, only one Roman scheduled monument appears on the schedule ... [However] From 1924–28 there seems to have been a flurry of activity concerning the scheduling of Roman remains' (Robertson 2000, 29) On the assumption that the first priority of the Victorians was to preserve the exotic 'other', then perhaps the scheduling of Roman monuments in the interwar period indicates an awareness that Roman civilisation was not quite so familiar as had previously been thought.

Both Acts were actively enforced during the interwar period. There seems to have been a growing recognition during this period that the protection of ancient monuments is a responsibility of the state (Robertson 2000, 49). Between 1913 and 1933 the number of sites placed in guardianship under the Act of 1882 rose from 44 to 273; the number of sites scheduled under the 1913 Act rose from 344 in 1921 to 3,195 in 1932 (Sheail 1981, 49). However, the shortcomings of the 1882 and 1913 Acts had already been realised for some time. In 1920 a committee set up to consider amendments to the Acts had concluded that, contrary to popular opinion, 'the Nation's interest in and consequent duty towards National monuments is far behind what is embodied in the legislation of other countries' (in Morris 2007, 300).

Unfortunately, this warning was ignored and archaeologists working on Hadrian's Wall were only too well aware that neither of these acts had been able to prevent damage to the Wall through quarrying. They also realised that although the Wall itself was now scheduled, this was of no use if a quarry might legitimately destroy its immediate surroundings. Already in 1929 the Ancient Monuments Committee of the Society of Antiquaries of Newcastle had agreed upon the need for 'parliamentary action to remedy defects in existing protective legislation' (*PSAN* 4, 192).

The plans for the new quarry necessitated that this need should now be communicated to the wider world.

The latest threat to the Wall originated in the terms of an agreement, dated 12 July 1929, between Sir Hugh Blackett and Mr John Frederick Wake, a Darlington engineer who already had an interest in the quarry at Cawfields. By this agreement, Wake leased the mineral rights between the Wall and the Vallum within a 5-mile stretch of land between milecastle 42 and turret 37A – the most spectacular stretch of the Whin Sill. In this area, according to the conditions of his lease, he was entitled to quarry within 10 feet of Hadrian's Wall. Along this stretch of the Wall the ground falls steeply away to the north but to the south the ground slopes gently downhill. As *The Times* pointed out, the result of the quarrying would be to leave the Wall no longer on a wave crest but upon a knife-edge. In effect, it would be removed from its original position in the landscape.

Mr Wake had also bought Hotbank Farm, immediately to the north of the Wall, from Sir Hugh Blackett (P.R.O. WORKS 14/1257). Although the plans for quarrying on this land were less pressing, this meant that the Wall faced a potential threat from both the north and the south.

An initial perusal of the numerous letters and articles in the press on this subject gives the impression of a spontaneous outburst of protest. One typical letter, from a group of ramblers, recently returned from the Wall, asked, 'Is it not possible to leave this imperial monument for the curlews to haunt and for time alone to destroy?' (*The Times* 22 April 1930).

Will Cadby of Shrewsbury was exceptional in taking a more utilitarian view:

> England is not yet a 'museum piece,' but the home of 40-odd millions of people, who surely should take precedence of any antiquity, and the idea that much useful productive work and employment should be turned down with a howl of disapproval because those of us who have time to visit this remote district may lose some aesthetic pleasure argues an insincerity in our view of the tragic social problems of the present day. (*The Times* 22 April 1930)

Yet, notwithstanding the large element of spontaneous indignation at the threat to the Wall, behind the protests there was – as will be seen – a considerable degree of co-ordination.

A Very Serious Matter

The earliest record on file concerning the proposed quarry is a letter dated 11 January 1930, from Parker Brewis to Joscelyn Bushe-Fox, the Inspector of Ancient Monuments, who, prior to the war, had excavated as a student on Hadrian's Wall at Corbridge:

Dear Bushe-Fox,

... I have just heard, on fairly good authority, that one of the purchasers at the Clayton Sale intends to start quarrying near Peel Crag. This is a <u>very</u> serious matter. The mineral rights in this portion do not belong to the surface owner, but to the Blacketts. I wish you could do something in this matter, at once, for if once a new quarry gets under way, I do not see how it can be stopped – and this is one of the most picturesque portions of the Wall ...

Parker Brewis (P.R.O. WORKS 14/1257)

Having discovered further details about the proposed quarry, Parker Brewis evidently discussed his concerns with Wake in person and then, again, passed on his findings to Bushe-Fox:

19.02.30

Dear Bushe-Fox,

... I found him [Wake] to be an intelligent gentleman who had travelled over Europe, Asia and America, and who had spent 2 years in planning the proposed quarry. He means to get it going, with your sanction, if possible but if he cannot get this, will start without it – for he has already spent 30,000 pounds on the matter.

Parker Brewis (P.R.O. WORKS 14/1257)

On 28 February, Parker Brewis discussed the matter with Charles Peers, Chief Inspector of Ancient Monuments (and architect of the 1913 Ancient Monuments Act). In a letter from Parker Brewis to Peers dated 1 March it is revealed that the Principal of Armstrong College in Newcastle (then part of Durham University) favoured writing to the press. However, in a letter to Peers dated 3 March (P.R.O. WORKS 14/1257), Parker Brewis argues that for the

moment those concerned should refrain from alerting the press: at this stage
he was still hopeful that the matter might be settled by private negotiation.

On 5 March, at a meeting of the Society for the Promotion of Roman
Studies at Burlington House in London, Parker Brewis apprised the Society's
president, Professor F. E. Adcock of Cambridge University of the full gravity of
the situation. Then on 7 March he again met Peers (P.R.O. WORKS 14/1257).

As is apparent from the following letter from Parker Brewis to Peers, by
2 April hope of a privately negotiated settlement had faded:

My dear Peers,

Yesterday [2 April 1930] a few of us had a meeting and discussed the Wall.
There is a strong feeling that our local press is soulless, carrying no weight
and that the 'Times' does not like to print after the lesser fry, that therefore
we had better open with an official letter from our Society [the Society
of Antiquaries of Newcastle upon Tyne] to the Times, or one by Sir Geo.
MacDonald primed up by us. I enclose draft for discussion. Can you return
it with any comments in time for Monday's meeting? If the Government
cannot at once strengthen the Ancient Monuments Act, do you think they
would pass a short Act dealing solely with the Roman Wall? Making Peel
Crag eastwards past Housesteads a national park. If you had Housesteads
as Headquarters for a couple of men to patrol the Wall, you might also get
Chesters Fort. As you know Chesters Museum is another problem. The
contents may have to come to Newcastle. We might also get the Duke's
Roman stones and have a really fine Roman Wall Museum here. It is all part
and parcel of the same matter. Could we not get the Rockefeller or Carnegie
Trust to help financially and do something really great?

Yours truly,

Parker Brewis (P.R.O. WORKS 14/1257)

Such was the background to the letter of protest that appeared in *The Times*
on 11 April. It was only after it became apparent that there was no hope of
Peers and Wake negotiating a settlement in private that the campaign was
brought to the attention of the national press.

A Need for New Legislation

It is noticeable that Parker Brewis' attitude in his letter of 3 April to Peers is quite different from that of his previous letters – and not just for the reason that hope of a private settlement had disappeared. It carries a new tone of confidence and ambition – to 'do something really great'. Bearing this in mind, it seems likely that it was at the previous day's meeting that a semi-official conservationists' committee was formed – the existence of which was later acknowledged in the pages of the *Journal of Roman Studies* (*JRS* 1930, 125). From the start, the committee hoped that the threat to the Wall might, with public backing, be turned into an opportunity to better protect it in the future.

The files in the public record office reveal something of the organisation behind the conservationists' campaign. The campaign was two-pronged: on the one hand it was focused upon the correspondence pages of the national press; and, on the other hand, it kept up 'behind-the-scenes' negotiation. The conservationists' committee at the hub of the protest consisted of the Cambridge historian and president of the Society for the Promotion of Roman Studies Professor F. E. Adcock; the Scottish archaeologist Sir George MacDonald (who, among other duties, held a post at the Carnegie Trust); the archaeologist and philosopher R. G. Collingwood; R. E. M. Wheeler; and Parker Brewis (chairman of the Newcastle Society of Antiquaries' Ancient Monuments Committee).

Of the five members, most (if not all) had already known each other for many years. MacDonald, Parker Brewis and Collingwood were experts on the Wall, and were fully alert to the archaeological importance of the land in question; but it was probably Collingwood and Wheeler who had the most experience of conservationist campaigns. Collingwood was brought up in a household in which conservation issues were frequently discussed. His father W. G. Collingwood was a member of the Lake District Defence Society (which in some respects can be regarded as the prototype of the National Trust) and in 1912 father and son had successfully campaigned for funds to buy Ambleside Roman fort on behalf of the National Trust.

Little is known of Wheeler's part in the campaign. Possibly, as Collingwood and Wheeler were friends, it was Collingwood who had persuaded Wheeler to join the committee. Certainly having Wheeler on board would have made sense, for Wheeler, whose father was a journalist, had recent experience of harnessing the power of the press to the cause of conservation: in 1926 he had famously persuaded the *Daily Mail* to buy the amphitheatre at Caerleon, in order to preserve it from development.

Adcock, likewise, is not generally known for any association with Hadrian's Wall – though the Chesters visitors' books testify to his presence on the Wall at this time. But, as president of the Society for the Promotion of Roman Studies, it was on his watch that the danger threatened. Like Collingwood and Parker Brewis, Adcock had worked for Admiralty Intelligence during the war – and is believed to have been responsible for recruiting Alan Turing to the intelligence community in the Second World War. (Adcock features as a character in Robert Harris' *Enigma*, under the name F. J. Atwood.) His contemporaries knew him as 'spruce and slightly fussy'; a *bon viveur* and a player of 14-hole golf; and, also, a sore loser (see Richmond 2001 & 2002). In his work as a historian, he was sometimes criticised for recognising only the forces of *realpolitik*. In the battle to save Hadrian's Wall, he would now have opportunity to practise these arts at first hand.

Parker Brewis would have found Peers, the Inspector of Ancient Monuments, most sympathetic to the suggestion that the conservation of Hadrian's Wall should be dealt with not in a piecemeal fashion, but via an all-encompassing scheme. Already in a letter of 21 February 1928, dealing with problems of erosion at Corbridge, Peers had declared that he would like to see 'a comprehensive scheme of State Maintenance of the Wall'. However, he confessed that he thought it unlikely that he would live to see such a scheme (Northumberland Record Office SANT/ADM/5/1/1). (Peers' own part in this and many other conservation campaigns would be recognised in 1931 when he received a knighthood.) The conservationists seem to have taken a pragmatic attitude as to whether a conservation scheme should best be undertaken via the National Trust or via the Office of Works (the forerunner of English Heritage) or whether the Carnegie and Rockefeller Foundations should be involved. However, they were agreed that the only ultimately satisfactory solution to the perpetual problems of conservation would be one on a grand scale – in Parker Brewis' words, 'something really great', for already at this date the Wall was seen, in modern terms, as a *world* heritage site. In sum, although there was undeniably a grave threat to the wall, there was also a perceived opportunity to respond to the threat upon a grand scale. After its opening clarion call, the next day – 12 April – *The Times* returned to the theme:

This is by no means the only instance of a state of affairs which points to a need for new legislation. Early British earthworks and other monuments on the headland of Penmaenmawr are being blotted out by quarrying operations.

It was suggested in a responsible quarter yesterday that the Rural Amenities Bill now before Parliament may offer the most practicable means of safeguarding the setting of important ancient works. The Bill has yet to be considered in Committee, but it already goes a considerable way towards widening the powers of local authorities in such rural areas as that in which the threatened part of the wall is situated. It is suggested that these authorities should be given powers for regional town planning of land adjoining a national monument, and so be enabled to forbid development of any kind that would impair the value of the monument.

Mr. R.D. Denham will ask the Prime Minister in the House of Commons on Tuesday [15 April] whether his attention has been called to proposed quarrying operations to the south of the Roman Wall, and whether he will cause a Select Committee to be appointed to advise the House as to the desirability of taking immediate steps to preserve the land between the Wall and the Vallum from destruction. On Monday [14 April] Sir Kingsley Wood will ask the First Commissioner of Works whether he proposes to take any action on the matter.

The Times then quoted in full the resolution that had been passed unanimously the previous day at the concluding session of the Classical Association's meeting at Hull University College. The resolution, moved by Canon Richards of Durham,

calls on the Government to take immediate action to save our greatest Ancient Monument from being disfigured and rendered well nigh inaccessible ... The exploration of the Roman Wall had reached a stage at which attention was concentrated not so much on the line of the Wall as on the ground in its immediate vicinity. Within a few miles south of the Wall lay the point to which the attention of the excavators was at present directed ... In the end, if the project was allowed to be carried out, the Wall would be perched on the top of a cliff overlooking a precipice, the whole appearance of the ground would be changed, and it would no longer be even easy to approach the Wall.

There was also a letter from Charles Peers, writing as President of the Society of Antiquaries of London. Peers wrote as follows:

It cannot be too strongly emphasized that the untouched nature of the surroundings of large stretches of the Wall forms a setting without which the Wall itself becomes a mere specimen of Roman engineering rather than a living memorial of history ... It is said, Sir, that the project which threatens the surroundings of the Wall is one which in these difficult days will provide employment and bring no small measure of prosperity to the North, and that it must not be set aside for what are often called 'sentimental' reasons. The matter is one of values. Can we afford to sacrifice this part of our national heritage for a material gain? Shall we be the richer or the poorer by so doing? I think that there can be but one answer, and am confident that I am not alone in that opinion.

In the same day's *Times* John Bailey, chairman of the National Trust's executive committee, pointed out that scheduling alone did not amount to a guarantee of a monument's conservation:

All that is secured for it is a respite. If the owner proposes to 'demolish, remove, structurally alter, or make additions' to it he must give notice to the Commissioner of Works and must not begin any such work for a month. During this brief respite the Commissioners may make a Provisional Order for its preservation, which remains in force for 18 months. But after that, unless money is granted by Parliament for purchase or compensation, the owner is enabled to act as he pleases.

It is obvious, therefore, that the protection afforded is of the most limited character; and all who care for our historic monuments will desire, with you, that the hands of the Office of Works should be strengthened so as to enable them to give these buildings a real and permanent, instead of this temporary and almost illusory, security.

But the security is not merely temporary. It is also only partial. To preserve, say, Fountains Abbey, and allow a factory to be erected 50 yards away from it, is a mockery and an absurdity. That is, in effect, what will happen to the Roman Wall if the scheme of the promoters is allowed to go through. But we earnestly hope that, even at this eleventh hour, by the assistance of your protest, and perhaps by Parliamentary intervention some means may be found of averting so great a catastrophe. It is not too much to say that if this cannot be done the beauty and interest of the Wall will be lost in a wilderness of cable transports, steel buildings and galvanized roads.

One other word. The promoters claim that their scheme would find work for a certain number of men. No doubt it would; and at a time like the present no one can speak lightly of the employment problem. But even to-day we may ask, and are surely bound to ask, what the workers are to be employed in, and whether their work is of to nature to injure and not to benefit the country. It would give employment to build a row of factories in Hyde Park; but nobody proposes to do it.

Questions were asked in the House of Commons (*The Times* 15 April 1930); and throughout this month letters of protest continued to appear in the correspondence columns of all the major national newspapers.

Explaining not only the importance of the Wall's conservation but also the level of protest, the historian George Trevelyan noted the increasing numbers of visitors to the Wall:

The study of Roman Britain, conducted under great archaeologists like Haverfield and his successors, has become a principal part of our historical science and our popular culture. The number of visitors to, and walkers along, the Wall is increasing by leaps and bounds. (*The Times* 16 April 1930)

The increase in visitor numbers since the First World War is confirmed by the Chesters visitors' books, which include, on 21 August 1924, the signature of

Queen Mary. (The archaeologist R. C. Bosanquet, who acted as the Queen's guide, was later singled out for praise for his role in successfully negotiating the transfer of the museum's exhibits, from Jack Clayton to the nation.) (*JRS* 1931, 125)

Trevelyan suggested that the increase in visitor numbers was partly attributable to Kipling's *Puck of Pook's Hill* (1906) and this indeed seems likely. The stories that comprise *Puck of Pook's Hill* were written from 1904, when Kipling had been a regular guest of the Straker family of Stagshaw House near Corbridge (Rivet 1978). W. G. Collingwood alludes to Kipling's work in his guide to Ambleside:

> I hope to meet the British tripper, not unwelcome, enjoying the treat provided him by enlightened Ambleside, and in the ramparts of the ancient Romans reading to his wife and children the story of Parnesius the centurion [a character in *Puck of Pook's Hill*]. (Collingwood 1912, 15)

R. G. Collingwood's guides to the Wall would also have played a part in the increase in visitor numbers. For not only did Collingwood summarise the latest archaeological finds but he located the best scenery on the Wall and the whereabouts of local hotels, pubs and guesthouses. Likewise, the text and illustrations of Jessie Mothersole's evocative *Hadrian's Wall* (1922), written with the advice of Wall archaeologists so as to make the latest archaeological discoveries understandable to the widest possible audience, would have contributed to visitor numbers.

Within a wider context, it should be remembered that this was the early heyday of what has been dubbed the British Outdoor Movement (Taylor 1997) – with day-trippers enjoying the countryside in ever-greater numbers. In response to this phenomenon, 1930 saw the official beginning of the youth hostel association of England and Wales (with George Trevelyan as the first president).

But day-trippers in motorcars would of course have added to the demand for better roads; and ironically it was this demand for better access that had made the Melkridge quarry a potentially profitable business venture in the first instance. The potential for conflict between access and conservation was realised at the time: for example, Collingwood ruefully noted that since it had been taken over by the National Trust it was no longer permitted to camp on Peel Island, as it had been in his childhood (Collingwood 1940, 32). In *Outlines of a Philosophy of Art* he had remarked that 'the love of the picturesque is a self-contradictory attitude and one which is bound to destroy what it loves by the very fact that it loves it' (Collingwood 1925, 62).

Yet still the archaeologists welcomed public interest in the Wall. Indeed, one of Collingwood's express concerns at the break-up of the Clayton estate was that public access to the Wall would henceforth be restricted. (Taylor and Collingwood 1929, 185). As will be seen, the archaeologists' engagement with the public would ultimately work to the benefit of the Wall's protection.

Mr Lansbury's Visit

On 17 April, *The Times* announced that the First Commissioner of Works, Mr George Lansbury, would visit the Wall to assess the situation for himself:

Mr. Lansbury's Visit Next Week
(from our special correspondent)
Newcastle-upon-Tyne, April 16
   Details have been received here today of the visit which Mr. George Lansbury, the First Commissioner of Works, intends to make to Hadrian's Wall next Wednesday [23 April 1930]. He will be accompanied by two members of the staff of the Office of Works, Messrs Peers and Raby [Dr Frederick J. E. Raby, Fellow of the Society of Antiquaries, specialist in medieval Latin poetry and assistant secretary to HM Office of Works], and will motor from Newcastle on Wednesday morning to Housesteads. The Town Clerk of Newcastle will accompany the party.
   Mr. Lansbury states that there is a wrong impression in the public mind that the actual Roman Wall itself would be demolished if the projected quarrying operations are allowed to be undertaken. This, of course, is a misapprehension. Neither the Wall nor the dyke can be touched as they enjoy protection as ancient monuments. 'It is,' Mr. Lansbury says, 'one thing to protect an ancient monument, but quite another thing to prevent anyone carrying out industrial operations anywhere near it. We want to do everything possible to preserve this historic Roman relic and its immediate surroundings, and the object of my visit to the Wall will be to ascertain at first hand what is practicable.'

The paper then went on to relay the opinions of the Wall archaeologist F. G. Simpson. (Many years later Grace Simpson recalled that the conservation of the central section of the Wall was her father's main preoccupation at this time (Simpson 1976, 11).)

   Mr. Simpson and the Quarry Scheme
      Mr. F. Simpson, a member of the council of the Society of Antiquaries on Newcastle-upon-Tyne, and who for many years has been engaged on research

work on the line of the Roman Wall, has replied to the statement of Mr. Wake, son of Mr. J.F. Wake, the engineer and quarry owner of Darlington, that the proposed quarry operations at Melkridge, near the Roman fort of Housesteads, would not injure the Wall. Mr. Simpson said nothing had taken place that could alleviate the fears of the antiquaries. The protest which had appeared was based upon an official memorandum of conversations between Mr. Wake and representatives of the Office of Works and the Newcastle Society of Antiquaries. With regard to the supposed unique qualities of the stone, Mr. Simpson did not make any statement.

He said the public would notice that the supply of stone was described as inexhaustible. The statement obviously foreshadowed an extension of the quarrying operations. The statement had been made that the more important view of the Roman Wall was on the north, while the quarrying will be on the south. Every archaeologist knew that the important view was east and west, while it was almost inevitably approached from the south. While the Wall itself might not be touched, the Military Way would of necessity be totally destroyed. Did Mr. Wake know that there was no wall standing where he proposed to begin operations? True there was no wall above the ground, but the highest existing stretch of wall, 9ft high, was completely covered until it was unearthed.

Mr. Simpson urged that such a large scale production, once begun, would have to go on from Shield-on-the-Wall to those danger spots where alone the so-called inexhaustible supplies could be found

Mr. Wake contends that the Roman Wall does not touch the quarry area and that the stone is to be used for road making. If his scheme goes ahead he intends to open works on the Tyne for the disposal of the broken stone.

From the outset of the affair there was little doubt where *The Times'* sympathies lay, but what of George Lansbury's?

George Lansbury is probably best remembered today not as the First Commissioner of Works but as the Christian pacifist leader of the Labour Party in the wake of Ramsay MacDonald's resignation on 23 August 1931. However, in April 1930, when the threat to the Wall was first made public knowledge, Lansbury was First Commissioner of Works in Ramsay MacDonald's second short-lived Labour government. His biographer describes him at this time, aged seventy, as

large-framed … with white hair and ruddy face adorned by mutton-chop whiskers, attired in an old alpaca suit and bowler hat. Instantly recognised wherever he went, he possessed an unmistakable ringing voice, in which he greeted everyone as his friend. (Shepherd 2002, 1)

According to A. J. P. Taylor, Lansbury was simply 'the most lovable figure in modern politics' (Taylor, 191 fn3).

In his autobiography, the Chancellor of the Exchequer, Philip Snowden, suggests that there was initially a distinct lack of enthusiasm for finding Lansbury a Cabinet position of any kind. However, since he had been conspicuously absent from the Cabinet of the first Labour government an obligation was felt to find him a post of some kind. It was finally decided that the position of First Commissioner was that in which he would do least harm. As Snowdon explains:

> What to do with Lansbury was something of a problem. He had been kept out of the previous Labour Cabinet, but we all agreed that some Cabinet office would have to be found for him in the new Government. But we also agreed that he could not be put in as head of an important Department. Merited, or unmerited, the stigma of 'Popularism' still clung to him. I suggested that he might be given the Office of Works. I thought this post would suit him admirably. He would not have much opportunity for squandering money, but he would be able to do a good many small things which would improve the amenities of Government buildings and the public parks. (In Shepherd 2002, 256)

Lansbury may have landed the position of First Commissioner as a means of damage limitation, but from the start he took the responsibilities of the post very seriously. One of his first actions as First Commissioner had been to travel to Skara Brae in the Orkneys in August 1929, to see for himself the threat posed by the elements to Gordon Childe's newly discovered Neolithic village. According to Lansbury's biographer, from then on the inspection of Skara Brae 'became a regular annual outing for First Commissioners and, to this day, part of Skara Brae is known as "Lansbury's Gallery"' (Shepherd 2002, 270).

In London, two of Lansbury's more controversial innovations as First Commissioner were to allow public access to the gardens of some of London's squares and to grant permission for mixed bathing in the Serpentine. Despite fears expressed in the press at the time, the threat to public order posed by the latter measure proved unfounded.

That a socialist government might be insufficiently concerned with the preservation of the nation's heritage was a fear that was also soon to be dispelled. In the 1880s, opposition to Sir John Lubbock's Ancient Monuments Bill had come mainly from the Conservatives, anxious to protect private property rights, but by 1930 the issue of conservation seemed to cut across party lines. Indeed, before the controversy broke, on 8 May 1929 on the eve of the general election, Stanley Baldwin, Ramsay MacDonald and Lloyd George had a letter published in *The Times* in which they declared:

> During the next few weeks we shall differ on so many problems of public importance, that we gladly take an opportunity of showing that on one subject we speak with a united voice – namely in advocating the preservation of our countryside in its rich personality and character.

Arguably, it was Baldwinite Conservatism that seemed most out of tune with the dramatic regulation and planning that the unforeseen crisis on Hadrian's Wall seemed to call for (see Matless 1998, 30). But, as will be seen, the party leaders' resolution to speak with a united voice would, in the face of this unexpected test, remain unbroken.

It was Parker Brewis, in communication with Peers, who made the arrangements for Lansbury's visit. In the course of making these arrangements, in one of his letters to Peers (dated 15 April 1930), Parker Brewis makes an interesting revelation:

> When I wrote to the Editor of the 'Times' I told him that if this work were stopped compensation might be the crux of the whole affair & might lead to a settlement by compromise, such as the preserving of the best bits at a cost of allowing the less perfect stretches to be quarried, but I asked him not to mention this. (P.R.O. WORKS 14/1257)

Although convinced of the importance of conserving the Wall, Parker Brewis was never dogmatic. His publicly stated demands exceeded his expectations, although to what extent Parker Brewis spoke here on behalf of the rest of the conservationists' committee is not known.

A final letter from Parker Brewis to Peers, dated 18 April, took care of the travel arrangements:

> I think you had best all three [Lansbury, Peers and Raby] pack into the back of my car, my chauffeur and I being in front. If we hire a second car we should possibly get separated somewhere. (P.R.O. WORKS 14/1257)

According to plan, Lansbury, Peers and Raby duly left King's Cross at 5.30 p.m. on Tuesday 22 April, staying that night in the Central Station Hotel in Newcastle. The next morning was fine and sunny, and the party left the hotel at 10.00 a.m. (half an hour later than planned).

Accompanied by Mr A. M. Oliver, Town Clerk of Newcastle (presumably in a separate car), they drove first of all to Limestone Corner. (*Evening World* 23 April 1930, *Northern Echo* and *Daily Telegraph* 24 April 1930) They were followed by a slew of pressmen, including representatives of the *Evening World*, the *Leeds Mercury*, the *Northern Echo*, the *Daily Mail*, the *Manchester Guardian*, the *Daily Telegraph* and *The Times*. Consequently, from the reports of these papers, it is possible to build a quite detailed account of the events of that day.

Having inspected the ditch north of the Wall at Limestone Corner the party then travelled on to the fort of Housesteads. To emphasise the remoteness of the fort's position, one journalist recorded that, as they approached the fort, they met a country postman whose daily round was no less than 23 miles.

At the fort itself they were greeted by the 'bronzed and white-bearded figure' (*Evening World* 23 April 1930) of the fort's caretaker and guide (for the past forty-eight years (Birley 1961, 294)), Mr Thomas Thompson, aged eighty-one (*Northern Echo* 24 April 1930). Mr Thompson collected the group's sixpences and took Mr Lansbury to his hut to sign the visitors' book.

'It would be a bad job indeed,' said Mr Thompson, 'if any harm was to come to the Wall after all these years' (*Northern Echo* 24 April 1930).

'Do your best, governor!'

'We will,' replied Lansbury (*Evening World* 24 April 1930).

Also at the fort were William Straker of the Northumberland Miners' Federation and R. J. Taylor, chairman of the Haltwhistle Labour Party. Taylor emphasised the needs of the unemployed in the district, pointing out that the quarry would give employment to 500 men. This was an argument that – at the depth of the Great Depression – obviously held great weight. Lansbury conceded as much.

> 'That point of view is one that the Government must take into account,' said Mr Lansbury. 'But why must you come to this particular part of the wall for your quarry?'
>
> 'Because it is here that lies the best stone,' replied Mr Taylor.
>
> 'But I can visualise a company being floated and the whole countryside laid open and spoiled if this proposed quarry scheme goes through,' said

FATE OF THE ROMAN WALL.

MR. LANSBURY MEETS THE OLD KEEPER.

Mr. Lansbury chatting with the old custodian of the Roman Camp at Housesteads. The old man is Mr. Thomas Thompson, aged 81, and he has kept guard over the Roman wall for over 50 years. (By a " Mercury " photographer.)

1.3. Lansbury and Thomas Thompson. (*Leeds Mercury*)

Mr Lansbury. 'Everybody is agitated about this matter, even in London. The argument that it is the best stone here is not enough reason, in my opinion, to spoil the countryside.' (*Daily Telegraph* 24 April 1930)

Parker Brewis gave the conservationists' view – that quarrying would leave the site perched upon a 400 foot-high pinnacle bearing no relation to its original situation. He also gave a general tour of the site – an experience that Lansbury seemed to genuinely enjoy.

'One would have thought you had lived here,' he remarked.
Parker Brewis' comments on the defensive role of the Wall, prompted another jocular response: 'Nothing on God's earth could keep Scotsmen out of England. They always want to rule us' (*Daily Mail* 24 April 1930). Parker Brewis then pointed out the wheel marks of the Roman vehicles that entered the fort:

'The wheel marks are 4ft. 8½ins. apart,' said the antiquary, 'and it is said that Stephenson measured that distance and made it the gauge of the railway lines. However, that may or may not be true.' (*Northern Echo* 24 April 1930)

Their tour of Housesteads completed, the party followed the Wall towards the west over the contested ground. Looking back towards the east, Parker Brewis pointed out the King's Crag at Sewing Shields, where King Arthur and his Knights were said to sleep – to be awoken only if an old bugle was blown and a sword unsheathed at the same time. Mr Lansbury replied, in good humour though at somewhat of a tangent, that this reminded him 'of a story he had heard of a mountain that jumped over another mountain because both were in love with a river' (*Northern Echo* 24 April 1930).

After a picnic lunch, on the threatened ground leading up to the Wall, the party walked on towards Shield on the Wall, where it was proposed to start the quarrying.

At some point shortly after lunch, Mr Wake (plan in hand), and his solicitor, J. R. Hall, joined the party. Mr Wake explained that the Wall was not in any imminent danger and that he would not go nearer than 50 feet to the Wall.

'I think I have got it quite right,' said Mr Lansbury 'but if you floated a big company might not that knock all your plans into a cocked hat?'

'Mr. Lansbury,' replied Mr. Wake, 'there is no company going to work stone unless its situation can warrant it.' He explained that although it was planned to build a small electrical plant between the Vallum and the Wall the main plant would be a mile and a half away. Furthermore: 'The scheme will employ some hundreds of men.' (*Northern Echo, The Times* 24 April 1930)

1.4. Looking over the Wall. (*Northern Echo*)

MR. LANSBURY PONDERS.

CAN HE SAVE HADRIAN'S WALL?

1.5. Lansbury ponders. (*Daily Mail*)

Mr. LANSBURY waves to the Northern Echo photographer as he and his party have their lunch
[N.E.]

1.6. Picnic lunch. (*Northern Echo*)

1.7. Lansbury and Wake. (*Northern Echo*)

The rest of their conversation was carried on in private on their drive back to Newcastle, and then in the privacy of Lansbury's rooms at the Central Station Hotel (*Evening World* 23 April 1930).

Lansbury returned to London on the 4.30 p.m. train, 'confident that in the end we shall arrive at some sort of conclusion that will be satisfactory to all who desire to preserve that setting' (*History* 15, 237). However, 'there are 70 miles of wall, and possibly all cannot be preserved with the same zeal as the most important parts' (*Northern Echo* 24 April 1930).

Before he left he made a final statement to the press:

I am deeply grateful to Mr. Parker Brewis for the kind and informative way in which he has treated myself and those who accompanied me. I am deeply impressed with the amount of the Wall that is in a state of good preservation, and I think not only the people of this district but of the whole of Britain are to be congratulated on the fact that there was so public spirited a person as Professor George Trevelyan to secure for us Housesteads and the surrounding land, which are now held by the National Trust. I think if the whole of the land at present held by Mr. Wake under an option were to be treated as a quarry it would be in the nature of a national disaster.

This Wall and the whole of that countryside remain as history of a period which our children and our children's children will want to know about, and which they can only know about by being able to see the place as the Romans must have seen it all those years ago. I can quite understand Mr. Wake's position in the matter, and we have had a most friendly discussion about it and we are communicating with one another again. I expect we shall be meeting again. I cannot, of course, tell you what the basis of our discussions was but I feel confident that in the end we shall arrive at some sort of conclusion that will be satisfactory to all those who want to preserve the Wall and also the surrounding countryside.

Mr Wake is a really public-spirited citizen. He is a keen business man, but at the same time he does not want to be standing up against public opinion as a kind of Philistine. (*The Times* 24 April 1930)

Whatever his private doubts, Lansbury's equanimity and affable confidence in resolving the matter seem to have been genuine. Certainly his contemporaries, whatever their politics, respected the authenticity of his optimism and bonhomie. The newspapers give the impression that Lansbury took real pleasure in his day away from the Commons; and, when regaled while upon the Wall with the story of the sleeping King Arthur, Westminster must indeed have seemed very far away. Yet it was at Westminster that the fate of the Wall would be decided.

Resolutions of Protest

Despite Lansbury's apparent sympathy towards the conservation of the Wall, as the outcome of his visit was as yet unclear, there was no immediate let-up in the campaign of protest. Indeed, the day after Lansbury's visit *The Times* reported that the previous day a resolution of protest had been passed by the Cumberland and Westmoreland Society meeting in Carlisle (*The Times* 24 April 1930). (Unsurprisingly, R. G. Collingwood was at the meeting.) The protest had been sent to the Prime Minister and the leader of the Opposition (*CW*, 30, 219–20). Nothing was being taken for granted.

On 3 May, *The Times* reported that another letter of protest had been sent to the First Commissioner:

Hadrian's Wall
An Appeal from Oxford University
The following letter has been addressed to Mr. Lansbury, First Commissioner of Works, by members of Oxford University:–

University of Oxford, April 28

Sir,

As members of the University of Oxford, we venture to express to you the hope that some means may be found to limit the proposed extension of quarrying works in the immediate neighbourhood of Hadrian's Wall. The stretch of the Wall, together with its associated works the Vallum and the Military Way, running from Chollerford to Gilsland, is, in our opinion, one of the most valuable of our national monuments. Both its beauty and its significance have already been impaired by the existing quarries; and we feel that the time has come when a binding and permanent limitation should be imposed on further disfigurement. We realize the importance of providing work, to the extent at present contemplated, for unemployed men in the Newcastle district; but we submit that it would be disastrous to permit the unlimited extension of such works, and so to leave the way open for the eventual destruction of a great historical monument.

We are, Sir; your obedient servants,
GREY OF FALLODEN, Chancellor.

F. HOLMES DUDDEN, Master of Pembroke, Vice-Chancellor.
HUGH CECIL }   Burgesses
C.W.C. OMAN, Chichele Professor of Modern History } of the University
HERBERT L. WILD, Hon. Fellow of Exeter and formerly
Bishop of Newcastle.
H.A.L. FISHER, Warden of New College.
A.D. LINDSAY, Master of Balliol.
F.W. PEMBER, Warden of All Souls.
W.R. BUCHANAN RIDDELL, Principal of Hertford.
M.E. SADLER, Master of University College.
H.J. WHITE, Dean of Christ Church.
F.G.J. ANDERSON, Camden Professor of Ancient History.
GILBERT MURRAY, Regius Professor of Greek.
JOHN L. MYRES, Wykeham Professor of Ancient History and President of
the Royal Anthropological Institute.
CHARLES S. SHERRINGTON, Waynflete Professor of Physiology and
President of the Royal Society.
CYRIL BAILEY, Fellow of Balliol.
R.G. COLLINGWOOD, Fellow of Pembroke.

That Collingwood's name appears last on the list, coupled with the style of writing, strongly suggests that he was the main orchestrator of this particular protest – certainly, the signatories are all likely to have been known to him. A short letter dated 14 May, from Lansbury's official private secretary to the Prime Minister's private secretary makes it clear that the appeal from Oxford was also brought to the Prime Minister's attention:

Dear Mr Usher,
   I understand from Mr. Lansbury that the Prime Minister told him that he had not seen the representation from Oxford University published in the Times on the subject of the Roman Wall. I therefore send you a cutting which you may think it worth while to show to the Prime Minister.
Yours sincerely
R. Auriol Barker (P.R.O. WORKS 30/69/691)

The pressure from the conservationists was maintained when, on 8 May, the Prime Minister received the following letter from Professor Adcock.

Dear Prime Minister,
   I beg to submit to you, in the name of the signatories, the enclosed Memorial, in the hope that it may receive your favourable consideration. May I at the same time ask you permission to publish it in the public Press.

I am
Your obedient servant
F.E. Adcock
Professor of Ancient History
In the University of Cambridge
(P.R.O. WORKS 30/69/691)

On 15 May the Prime Minister granted Professor Adcock permission to publish his appeal and it duly appeared in *The Times* on 23 May under the heading 'Historians' Appeal to the Prime Minister':

In recent years Hadrian's Wall has become the center of a systematic enquiry which is being pursued along lines that have called forth the unstinted admiration of competent judges abroad as well as at home. Fruitful as this enquiry is proving to be, its ends are still a very long way from being accomplished. Unless the investigators are left unhampered, it can never achieve complete success. Nor would it be sufficient for their purpose that the structure of the Wall itself should be left severely alone. The belt of country immediately to the south of it contains forts and camps and other remains whose testimony would in due time be called for, but whose secrets will perish beyond hope of recovery, if the quarrying is allowed to proceed ...

Accordingly, we would most respectively urge His Majesty's Government to take such steps as may be necessary to ensure that the central portion of the line, including Wall and Vallum and the ground between them, together with reasonable margins north of the Wall and south of the Vallum, are placed under the guardianship of the Office of Works as an Ancient Monument, or are otherwise effectively protected by safeguards more binding and unalterable than the wishes of those, whether individuals or bodies, who may from time to time be in possession of the land, or of mineral rights over the land, on which the remains are situated.

Signed
F.E. Adcock, D. Litt., M.A., Professor of Ancient History in the University of Cambridge and President of the Society for the Promotion of Roman Studies
J.G.C. Anderson, LL.D., Camden Professor of Ancient History in the University of Oxford
B. Ashmole, M.A. Yates Professor of Archaeology in the University of London
D. Atkinson, M.A., F.S.A., Professor of Ancient History in the Victoria University of Manchester
N.H. Baynes, M.A., Reader in the History of the Roman Empire, University of London
T. Rice Holmes, D.Litt., Litt.D., F.B.A.

H. Stuart Jones, M.A., D.Litt., F.B.A., Vice-Chancellor of the University of Wales; formerly Camden Professor of Ancient History in the University of Oxford and President of the Society for the Promotion of Roman Studies
F.G. Kenyon, C.B.E., K.C.B., D Litt., L.L.D., F.B.A., Warden of Winchester College, Director and Principal Librarian, British Museum
G. MacDonald, K.C.B., D.Litt., F.B.A., formerly President of the Society for the Promotion of Roman Studies
J.W. Mackail, M.A., L.L.D., F.B.A., Professor of Ancient History in the Royal Academy
E.H. Minns, Litt.D., F.B.A., Disney Professor of Archaeology in the University of Cambridge
J.L. Myres, O.B.E., M.A., D.Sc., F.B.A., Wykeham Professor of Ancient History in the University of Oxford
H.A. Ormerod, M.C., M.A., Rathbone Professor of Ancient History in the University of Liverpool
Rennell Rodd, G.C.M.G., G.C.V.O., C.B.

A few days later, *The Times* published the British Academy's appeal to the Prime Minister signed by H. A. L. Fisher, one of the signatories of the appeal from Oxford University.

All the indications suggest that behind the scenes this was a highly organised campaign. It is a safe assumption that Collingwood and Adcock, and indeed every member of the conservationists' committee, were fully aware of each other's moves.

Reasonable Restrictions

Meanwhile, in a letter dated 9 May, George Lansbury alerted the Prime Minister to the fact that the quarry would yield 200,000 tons a year and employ 200 men (not 500 as had been claimed) and that a resolution, in favour of the quarrying, had been received from the local Labour party. Lansbury then set out his own provisional conclusions, as follows:

I was impressed by the fact that Mr. Wake had already carried his operations and his commitments to considerable length, (he has bought his sidings and his riverside site) and that if he were to be prevented from proceeding both he and the mineral owner would require very heavy compensation. I was equally impressed by the fact that the opening of this quarry would provide much needed employment in an area that was being badly hit by trade depression. Mr. Wake stated quite clearly that he has no chance, even if he were given a free hand, of quarrying within his own lifetime over a larger area than that shown pink on the map. This area is actually about 105 acres, but from what Mr. Wake told me, I gather that the quarries themselves would not cover such a large area. He has not been very precise on this point, and my impression is that he mentioned 40 acres. He seemed very willing to come to some arrangement on these lines although I was, of course, unable at that stage to discuss any details. It seemed to me, therefore, that if Mr. Wake could be definitely limited to an area beyond which he must not go, the amount of possible compensation would perhaps be brought within manageable compass, work would be found for the neighbourhood, and if legislation were promised for dealing with the remainder of the wall, even the archaeologists might feel that their claims had been reasonably met.

I do not necessarily mean that Mr. Wake should have an entirely free hand over this smaller area. It might be possible to impose some reasonable restrictions upon him in order to prevent the ultimate effect of his operations from being too unsightly. It might also be possible to restrict the area to the amount which could be quarried within the next 21 years [the period for which Mr Wake had leased the mineral rights from Sir Hugh Blackett]. There is the further consideration that no one can tell whether the quarry is likely to be so successful as Mr. Wake anticipates, and it might be sufficient to allow him to proceed provisionally for 21 years, at the end of which time the matter might be reviewed. In any case, my point is that as I cannot, so far as I can see, take any effective action except after a comparatively long period in which matters would have to remain in suspense, I really think that Mr. Wake should be told at once that he may proceed with the quarrying in the area coloured red on the understanding that it may be necessary to insist on certain restrictions. If this decision were conveyed to Mr. Wake there would then be time to consider properly what further legislative action is needed and on what lines the question of compensation either to Mr. Wake or to the owner of the mineral royalties should be dealt with.

As regards legislation, I am inclined to think that what would be needed would be the imposition of a proper development plan of the area with sufficient restrictions to guard the amenities of the Wall, but on this point I am seeking the advice of the Ministry of Health.

I am quite aware that the course I have suggested as regards Mr. Wake will probably not commend itself to the whole body of archaeological opinion in this and other countries, and I appreciate to the full the arguments in favour of the preservation of the historic setting of this important Monument. If the scheme for quarrying had not already reached such an advanced stage, and if the question of employment did not enter into it so directly, I should have liked to have been able to oppose it in its entirety. But Mr. Wake, in proposing to quarry was not doing anything that was not strictly proper and lawful, and I think you will agree that the House of Commons would take a strong exception to what would practically amount to retrospective legislation, restraining a man from carrying out his business, even though he were compensated.

I feel, therefore, that if the quarrying could be limited to a comparatively small area there would be a solution of the immediate difficulty and the way would be open to take effective steps by legislation to protect the surroundings of the remainder of the Wall. Such legislation would involve compensation, and in any case, Mr. Wake and the mineral owner will eventually have to be compensated unless they are given an entirely free hand.

I should like to know, therefore, whether you see any objection to my informing Mr. Wake at once that he can proceed with his quarrying scheme, but that the Government will not, under any circumstances, contemplate any quarrying beyond a certain area and may indeed insist on the quarrying being limited to a smaller area than that proposed. If, however, you think that quarrying should be prevented altogether, and that the matter is of such importance that it must be brought before the Cabinet, I will have the necessary memorandum prepared.

Yours truly,

George Lansbury (P.R.O. WORKS 30/69/691)

In short, Lansbury raises the prospect of new legislation whereby it would be impossible for such a problem to arise again. However, he sees no acceptable way to prevent work at the Melkridge quarry entirely without paying substantial compensation. He suggests limiting quarrying to less sensitive areas.

Both Lansbury and the archaeologists would have been aware that the threat posed to the environs of the Wall was not unique. A similar problem had lately arisen at Stonehenge. The land surrounding Stonehenge had only been saved from the threat of development after a public appeal for £35,000, launched by Stanley Baldwin and Ramsay MacDonald in a letter to *The Times* on 5 August 1927 (Sheail 1981, 52). A similar threat to land surrounding Avebury had been averted by the purchases of the archaeologist Alexander Keillor (Sheail 1981, 57–60).

Collingwood's friend, O. G. S. Crawford, had been involved in the Stonehenge campaign (Sheail 1981, 53; P.R.O. WORKS 14/488), and had argued, in an editorial in *Antiquity* in 1929, that 'conservation, not excavation, is the need of the day … conservation not only of purely archaeological features but of the amenities which gave them half their charm' (Crawford 1929, 3). Crawford then went on to call for the gradual acquisition of large tracts of archaeologically sensitive land:

> Though costly, such a scheme is not impracticable; the best areas are naturally those which are least valuable for agricultural purposes. Moreover the time for action is *now*, before the price of land is raised by the prospect of development. (Crawford 1929, 3)

As will be seen, at about the same time, Crawford was also petitioning the government in favour of the introduction of national parks.

The conservationists were attempting to deal with both the immediate threat to ancient monuments and their long-term security.

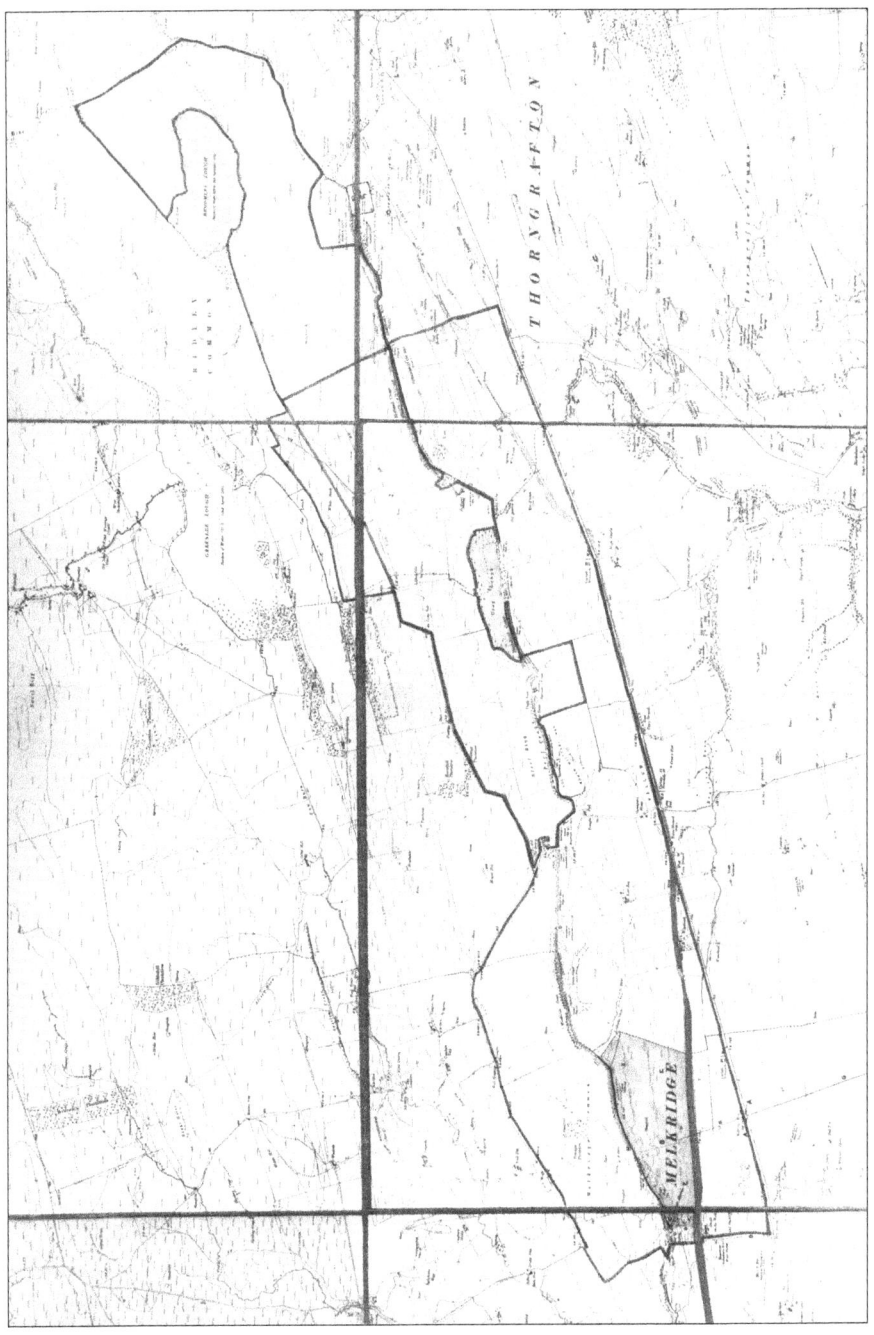

1.8 Land leased to Wake.

The Excellence of Good
Intentions for Paving Purposes

The legislation mentioned in Lansbury's memo to the Prime Minister was first discussed, at the Prime Minister's suggestion, at a meeting of the Cabinet on 28 May 1930 (P.R.O. WORKS 14/1257). Meeting no opposition, it was not long before the plans for new legislation were made public.

On 3 June 1930, reporting on the previous day's business in the Commons, *The Times* announced plans for a Bill to give protection to the surroundings of the Wall:

Hadrian's Wall
A Government Bill

Mr. Lansbury, First Commissioner of Works (Bow and Bromley), in reply to questions by Mr. Denman (Leeds Central, Labour) and Mr. A.W. Russell (Tynemouth, U) said:— The Government have given the proposed quarrying near Hadrian's Wall their most careful attention, and have come to the conclusion that, if the quarrying could be confined to a limited area, the result should be that no serious harm would be done, and the way be left open for the preservation of the surroundings of the remaining stretch of the Wall. Negotiations will proceed with this end in view. I should like to emphasize the fact that neither the wall nor the vallum is in any danger of being actually touched or damaged by the quarrying operations. At the same time, hon. Members will be glad to know that a Bill is in course of preparation which would give my Department adequate powers to protect the surrounding of ancient monuments including, of course, the Roman Wall. (Hear, hear.)

The same day F. G. Simpson conducted a party of two hundred, including the archaeologists R. G. Collingwood, O. G. S. Crawford, Sir George MacDonald, Parker Brewis, M. V. Taylor, and Mortimer and Tessa Wheeler, over the threatened section of the Wall. This was part of the decennial 'Pilgrimage' that over four days traversed the entire length of the Wall, from east to west. (When William Hutton traversed the Wall in 1801 he had doubted that anyone would ever again attempt such a feat, but in 1849 a group of antiquaries traversed the Wall – and termed their excursion a 'pilgrimage'. There followed pilgrimages, reviewing the intervening archaeological work on the Wall, in 1896, 1906 and 1920; but the fifth pilgrimage of 1930 was the largest yet.) It was on this occasion that it was resolved not to permit private cars to play so prominent a role in any future pilgrimage. According to the *Proceedings of the Society of Antiquaries of Newcastle* it was possibly the threat to the Wall that led to such a large turnout (*PSAN* 4, vii).

The pilgrims each carried a copy of Collingwood's *Book of the Pilgrimage* in which the latest archaeological research was summarised. No mention is made of the threat of quarrying in this book – perhaps for fear of upsetting negotiations – but the same year Collingwood published a second edition of his *Guide to Hadrian's Wall*, in which explicit reference is made to the threat posed by quarrying:

> The scenery, with its lakes, basalt crags, and distant views, is here at its best, and the remains of the Wall are very impressive, as they wind hither and thither to hold the edge of the crags or plunge into the gaps that separate one from the next. It is here, and for some distance to the west, that extensive quarrying operations are threatened, which if they proceed as planned, will destroy the finest piece of scenery on the Wall. (Collingwood 1930, 27)

Collingwood's concerns – first at the breakup of the Clayton estate and then at the threat of quarrying – were also expressed in his annual summaries of work completed in 'Roman Britain in 1929' (Taylor and Collingwood 1929, 185) and 'Roman Britain in 1930' (Collingwood and Taylor 1931, 219–20).

As the pilgrims passed the site of the new quarry at Melkridge it was noted that work had been suspended. However, the sight of the deep cutting into the Whin Sill (NY 72856685) and the destruction of a section of the Military Way (a road built in about AD 160 linking the Wall forts) would have been far from reassuring.

Not wanting to disturb negotiations, there seems to have been an agreement among the pilgrims to refrain from comment on the controversial new quarry – at least to members of the press. According to the Proceedings of the Cumberland and Westmorland Society:

> Speakers on the Pilgrimage refrained from references to the threatened invasion of the Wall's central and most impressive portions by a vast quarrying enterprise; but their audience knew that it was never long absent from their minds, and realised that, if the object of their pilgrimage was to be spared outrage, it could only be through the activity of a public opinion sufficiently widespread and sufficiently enlightened to enforce upon Governments the view that neither the enrichment of capitalists nor the employment of labour can justify the deliberate destruction of what ought to be regarded as one of the nation's chief treasures. (CWAAS, 31, 199–200)

However, immediately after the pilgrimage, Sir George MacDonald gave vent to his feelings in a letter published in the *Scotsman* on 7 July, later reprinted in

Antiquity (1930, 4, 358–61). MacDonald quoted Francis Haverfield's description of Winshields, the highest point of the entire Wall – for this too fell within the threatened section. (It was the place after which Haverfield, the co-ordinator of pre-war excavations on the Wall, had named his house in Oxford – such was his affection for it.) Here, in Haverfield's words, quoted by MacDonald:

> Nature and man combine in a unique landscape. As you look east and west, and trace the long line winding for miles from end to end of perilous ledges, and climbing from hill to hill, as you turn south to the Tyne and the dark fills beyond it, or north to long flat wastes and pathless mosses, the vision of a great empire rises. Here, on the uttermost limit of the Roman world, the desolate land has been stamped for ever with the sign of its former lords. On these high moors we can realize, almost more clearly than in the forum of Rome, the secret of that defence by which Rome guarded the fabric of civilization through the long menace of darkness and dissolution.

MacDonald went on to warn that

> the protesting voices that made themselves heard a few weeks ago have been far too easily lulled into silence ... I went to Newcastle with vaguely comforting rumours of negotiations ringing in my ears. I did my best to follow these up. But the nearer I got to the heart of things, the more nebulous did the negotiations become.

He spoke, in graphic terms, of the dire consequences that would follow should the protest fail:

> Unless the plague be stayed, the Pilgrims of 1940 will find that their way leads through the Valley of humiliation. It will be too late then to remember that at the end of this Valley is another, called the Valley of the Shadow of Death.

While the pilgrims, and the press, had been impressed by the summarised results of the previous ten years' systematic excavation, at Melkridge they had stared over the edge of the newly made cutting and into the abyss. Something of this discomfiting experience is conveyed in MacDonald's letter. That the environs of the Wall were regarded, by some, as expendable, was not a stimulus to archaeological excavation that would not otherwise have taken place. The confident and ambitious programme of archaeological research that was carried out between the wars required no such stimulus. Rather, the new quarry was seen as an intrusion into this research: it was, quite literally, a blasted nuisance.

As the parliamentary session drew to a close it became clear that Lansbury's Bill would not now be introduced until autumn. While the archaeologists had the government's full support for the conservation of the Wall's surroundings,

1.9. Cutting into the Whin Sill (NY72856685). (Alan Whitworth)

it was still necessary that public pressure be maintained, for the Bill was inevitably competing with a great deal of other business. In the hope that it would be pressed forward 'at the earliest moment', a long letter was published in *The Times* on 29 July, signed by Mr Rudyard Kipling, Professor Sir Charles Oman MP, the Right Hon. H. A. L. Fisher, Colonel Wedgwood MP, Mr John Buchan MP, Sir George MacDonald, and Sir Philip Pilditch:

> We all rejoice to know that the fort at Housesteads, together with the adjacent portion of the Wall, has been handed over to the National Trust. But there is reason for profound uneasiness as to what may happen to the finest section of all, the magnificent stretch which runs along the crags of the Great Whin Sill from Housesteads … to Carvoran. Hitherto it has been largely protected by the very loneliness which makes its surroundings so impressive. Near Carvoran, however, a quarry which was started on a modest scale many years ago, and which has already devoured a Roman mile-castle as the only alternative to leaving it standing alone on the top of a pillar of rock, is now within 100 yards of that part of the Wall which is most nearly in its original condition. It would be folly to shut one's eyes to the dangerous possibilities latent in the formation of a company bearing the ominous name of 'Roman Stone Limited,' and empowered to exploit the mineral rights over a large area to the west of Housesteads, up to and including the Wall, and between it and the Vallum. The building of motor roads throughout the country is giving an enormous stimulus to the demand for material. We have heard that the promoters speak of extracting 100,000,000 tons.

No doubt the working of the whinstone would give a much-needed fillip to employment in the district. But, as you yourself reminded your readers some weeks ago, there is abundance of equally suitable whinstone not very far away, while the volume of employment would not be lessened by a change. Nor need one question the sincerity of the promoter's disclaimer of any intention of attacking the Wall itself. We miss, however, any reference to the inevitable disfigurement of the adjacent landscape, and even in regard to the Wall the force of circumstance may prove irresistible. Is there not a homely proverb which testifies to the excellence of good intentions for paving purposes?

We understand that, although no sheds nor the threatened overhead means of transport have yet been erected, tentative operations have already been begun. What the public, we are sure, would like to have before Parliament rises is a statement from the First Commissioner of Works (as to whose sympathies we are assured) of the outcome of his negotiations with the promoters of the projected company. If he could supply for publication in your pictorial page, on which such a fine picture of the Wall itself at this point recently appeared, a plan showing exactly what he has been able to arrange, it might have the effect of allaying the apprehensions which are so widespread ...

Rudyard Kipling and John Buchan are not usually associated with archaeological conservation, but as can be seen from this letter they lent the campaign not only their names but also, quite possibly, their eloquence. In the House of Commons, George Lansbury tried to reassure the campaigners. On 1 August he replied to a question put by Sir J. Withers (MP for the University of Cambridge): 'No quarrying has yet begun on the site, and there will be no interference at any time with the Wall or the Vallum. If, as I hope, the legislation contemplated is carried through without delay, the surroundings of the Wall as a whole can be adequately protected for the future' (*History* 15, 238).

Nonetheless, leaving nothing to chance, the October issue of *History* urged its readers to write forthwith to their Members of Parliament (*History* 15, 239). The next session of Parliament was to open on the 28th of that month.

In the meantime, the Permanent Secretary of the Office of Works, Sir Lionel Earle, had drafted the Bill. In a memorandum dated 13 September, Earle highlighted the financial side of the problem. The Bill might be passed but there would still remain the problem of finding money to compensate those affected by its enforcement:

The Bill will provide effective means for protecting the surrounding of Ancient Monuments, but it cannot be too strongly emphasized that the whole crux of the problem is money for compensation. The Roman Wall will be the first case to be dealt with and it will be the most expensive. This is why we are taking provision to enable us to receive donations in aid from societies and individuals ... The question of the destruction of the countryside and of the beauty of our old towns appears to resolve itself into this. There is money readily available for destruction and no money for preservation ... (P.R.O. WORKS 30/60/91)

Having been read by the Prime Minister, on 3 November the draft Bill was presented by Lansbury to a large party of those whom had expressed their concern. The next day's *Times* recorded those who had been present at the meeting or who had sent letters of sympathy, including:

Mr. Rudyard Kipling, Mr. Stanley Baldwin, Lord Londonderry, Mr. Lloyd George, Sir Robert Hamilton, M.P., Lady Cynthia Mosley, all six members for the Universities of Oxford and Cambridge, the Northern Universities, and the University of London – namely, Sir Charles Oman, Lord Hugh Cecil, Sir John Withers, Mr. H. Wilson, Miss Rathbone, and Dr. Ernest Little – Lord Eustace Percy, Mr. H.A.L. Fisher, of the British Academy, Sir George MacDonald, of Edinburgh and the Roman Society, Mr. Parker Brewis and Professor Bosanquet, of the Society of Antiquaries of Newcastle-on-Tyne, Mr. F.G. Simpson, Director of Archaeology, Durham University, Lord Grey of Falloden and Mr. S.H. Hamer of the National Trust, Sir Emery Walker and Mr. Green, of the Society for the Protection of Ancient Buildings, Mr. Mortimer Wheeler, of the London Museum, Mr. R. Collingwood and Professor Anderson, of the Philological Society, Sir Reginald Blomfield, of the British Association, Mr. Francis Weston and Mr. Reginald Taylor, of the British Archaeological Association, Mr. Reginald Smith, of the British Museum, Sir Charles Trevelyan, Sir Nicholas Grattan-Doyle, Mr. J.H. Palin, Sir Philip Richardson, Mr. John Buchan, Sir Kenyon Vaughan-Morgan, Sir Martin Conway, Captain Bourne, Sir Douglas Newton, Major Isidore Salmon, Major Church, Major J.W. Hills, Mr. Philip Noel Baker, Sir Archibald Sinclair, Sir Albert Bennett, Mr. David Kirkwood, Mr. Andrew MacLaren, Mr. A.A. Somerville, Mr. E.J. St. Loe Strachey, Mr. H.C. Charleton, Sir George Berry, Mr. W.P.C. Greene, Mr. Isaac Foot, Mr. Arthur Hollins, Mr. Patrick Ford, Dr Vaughan Cornish and Professor Abercrombie.

Sir Philip Pilditch took the chair, and expressed the desire of those present of all parties to do all they could to help the First Commissioner in regard both to the possibilities of preventing the threatened injury to the prospect of the Wall by quarrying and also with regard to the proposed Bill for strengthening the Ancient Monuments Act.

Mr. Lansbury, the First Commissioner of Works, explained what he had been able to do on the first of these points, from which it appeared that the position was as satisfactory as might be expected, and that the Wall itself, which had been scheduled as an ancient monument, could not be touched nor the space within a certain number of feet of it, and that if any quarrying at all took place, which was by no means certain, it could touch neither the Wall nor the Vallum. With reference to the proposed Ancient Monuments Bill he asked those present for their promise to treat the matter as non-controversial, and he had every hope that on those lines he might get it passed this Session. The Bill aimed at removing some obscurities and defects in the existing Act, at providing machinery for the protection of the surroundings of ancient monuments, and, probably, for the control of the export of ancient buildings in whole or in part.

A number of those present in the course of the meeting asked questions and expressed the views of the societies they represented.

Lansbury's sincerity and interest in the matter seemed to impress even such sceptics as Sir George MacDonald. Nonetheless, in a note in *History*, MacDonald urged all those with any interest in the Wall to maintain pressure upon their MPs:

> The deputation which waited on the First Commissioner of Works at the opening of the parliamentary session was very favourably received. It is evident that Mr. Lansbury is genuinely interested. After making the actual position clear, perhaps as much by what he did not say as by what he did say, he sketched the main provisions of a Bill which had been drafted for the amendment of the Ancient Monuments Act. This Bill is now before Parliament, and it is safe to say that, had it been on the statute book a year and a half ago, the danger that still hangs over Hadrian's Wall could never have arisen. The proposed measure has warm supporters in all three parties, so that it is permissible to hope that it may pass by general consent. That is the one chance; and every reader of HISTORY should see to it that his or her local Member realizes the importance of maintaining a benevolent attitude. (*History* 1930, 325)

The Bill passed its second reading in the Lords on 11 December 1930 and finally became law on 11 June 1931. Its terms are set out in Appendix I.

Anticipating this event, the annual report of the Society for the Promotion of Roman Studies, dated 11 March 1931, makes the following reference to the part played by the conservationists' committee:

> A Committee consisting of the President [F. E. Adcock], Sir George MacDonald, Mr. R.G. Collingwood, Dr. R.E.M. Wheeler and Mr. Parker Brewis has taken an active part in the various measures by which it was sought to check the destruction of amenities threatened by a quarrying scheme. There has been introduced into Parliament a new Ancient Monuments Bill which will it is hoped, have received the Royal Assent before this Report is presented to the Society. The Committee are satisfied that when it becomes an Act, it should not only reduce the area of damage in this particular case, but should also strengthen very considerably the hands of those who are trying to preserve the Ancient Monuments of this country. (*JRS* 1930, 125)

The victory was commemorated in a ballad by Eric Birley, the new owner of Vindolanda.

A BALLADE OF CONSOLATION FOR THE
TRANSIENCE OF ALL HUMAN GLORY
AND RENOWN

When Hadrian ruled, the Roman sway,
Still strong, made every foeman shake,
From furthest Thule to Cathay;
Yet did that emperor forsake
Fresh conquest, and a barrier make –
A Wall – to bound his empire. True,
His day, long past, is dim, opaque,
But Hadrian's Wall is still on view.

Shakespeare, again, has had his day:
Who knows (or cares) what words he spake
On parting from Ann Hathaway?
Who knows what deeds Sir Francis Drake
Once did? Who suffered at the stake
In Good Queen Bess's time: or who
In Mary's burned, for conscience sake?
But Hadrian's Wall is still on view.

All creatures perish, and decay
O'ertakes Eve, Adam, and the Snake;
Man is but made of common clay
And soon must come to dust. You quake
At what's in store for you? Nay, slake
Your thirst, and take your fill anew:
You can't have and eat your cake,
But Hadrian's Wall is still on view.

Envoi

O Prince! O Quarryman! O Wake!
Don't think that I've forgotten you!
You may declare your heart will break,
But Hadrian's Wall is still on view!

Hadrian's Wall *was* still on view, but problems remained. As Collingwood pointed out (Collingwood and Taylor 1931, 220), the 1931 Act was not retrospective and so the quarries, until compensated, still had the legal right to remove stone until the end of their leases.

More Quarries Still

While the 1931 Act had made its way through Parliament, Raby had drawn up a preservation scheme (Charlton 2004, 6) but – in the depths of the Great Depression – it was not implemented, owing to the perennial matter of cost (P.R.O. WORKS 14/1124). Thus, despite funds having been offered by the Pilgrim Trust – a philanthropic trust established the previous year (John Buchan was one of the original trustees) – and despite Lansbury's successor, W. Ormsby Gore (First Commissioner of Works, November 1931 to May 1936) having persuaded many of the landowners to waive claims for compensation, there was still no official government-backed preservation scheme in place.

Sir Lionel Earle had argued that the government press on with the scheme on the grounds that the amount of compensation required would rise once the economy began to recover, but MacDonald's Chancellor of the Exchequer, Neville Chamberlain, had argued that no immediate action was required (P.R.O. WORKS 14/1259). (At one point, it was even proposed that the money that had been raised for the Hadrian's Wall preservation scheme be temporarily diverted in order to protect Avebury (Sheail 1981, 59).) As Sir Lionel Earle had pointed out, it was one thing to pass the Bill and quite another to find the money to implement it.

Fortunately, the threat to the Wall seemed to have abated: Wake had run out of capital (Sheail 1981, 54). But in principle the threat remained. Hence, in the 1933 edition of Collingwood's *Guide to the Wall*, the threat is not seen as having entirely disappeared. Of the area immediately west of Housesteads, Collingwood wrote:

> It was here, and for some distance to the west, that extensive quarrying operations were lately threatened, which, if they proceed as planned, will destroy the finest piece of scenery on the Wall. (Collingwood 1933, 27)

(A similar warning was added to Collingwood Bruce's *Handbook to the Wall*, edited by Collingwood.) Moreover, as mentioned, the new Act could not be applied retrospectively. That is to say, it could not overrule previously made legal agreements over mineral rights. The lease at Walltown ran until 1981;

Cawfields until 1943; and Wake's lease from Sir Hugh Blackett ran until 1949 but was renewable for a further twenty years (Charlton 1981, 59).

The upshot of this was that in 1937, when quarrying again threatened the Wall, the conservationists were again forced onto the defensive. At Greenhead, 300 yards of the Wall had recently been destroyed and a further half-mile faced imminent destruction, including turret 45a (Charlton 2004, 5); at Cawfields, the setting of milecastle 42 was threatened; however, the quarry at Melkridge remained dormant (Wright 1944, 75-7). This time, despite an illness that sometimes confined him to bed, it was Simpson, rather than Parker Brewis, who was the main intermediary between the Office of Works and the quarries, for Simpson, then the director of the Cumberland and Westmorland Antiquarian and Archaeological Society, tended to be more active in the west than Parker Brewis. Parker Brewis – who was awarded an OBE this year for his part in the earlier defence of the Wall (MacDonald 1940, 134) – was, besides, also suffering poor health (Simpson 1976, 7).

Although in 1932 Ramsay MacDonald had again joined forces with Sir George MacDonald, Collingwood, Wheeler and Peers – this time over a threat to Chester amphitheatre – by 1937 neither Ramsay, MacDonald nor Lansbury were in any position to play a role in the new crisis. Ramsay MacDonald, who had attracted the unforgiving opprobrium of his Labour colleagues by his part in the formation of the National government in 1931, had by now retired. Lansbury, no doubt in recognition of his response to the 1930-31 campaign, had been made honourable vice-president of the National Trust. But now, at the age of seventy-eight – having in the meantime taken over the leadership of the Labour Party in 1931 and been ousted in 1935 – he was fully engaged in visiting European leaders. On his own initiative, he was attempting single-handedly to avert the threat of war. He died in 1940.

Meanwhile, the number of visitors to the Wall had continued to grow. It has been estimated that there were approximately 15,000 visitors to Housesteads in 1935 (Woodside and Crow 1999, 94). A museum was built in 1936 to meet this demand. Thomas Thompson, now aged eighty-seven, was still employed as the caretaker of the fort – he died the following year (Birley 1961, 294) – assisted, since 1934, by his grandson William ('Billy') Thompson (Housesteads Minute Book 1930-49).

Frederick Raby was still at the Office of Works; and it was he who received Simpson at Storey's Gate at the start of December 1937. Simpson informed Raby that £2-3,000 must be paid to Colonel Joicey, the owner of Greenhead Quarry at Walltown in order to avert an imminent threat to the Wall and to Mucklebank Turret (turret 44b). According to the memo that Raby sent to the Treasury:

He [Simpson] has consulted with Prof. Collingwood and others, and apparently their idea was to approach the Rockefeller Foundation. It is said that the usual practice of this body, if it does contribute to such schemes, is to guarantee so much if more is forthcoming. It was with a view to ascertaining if any help could be expected from the Treasury via H.M.O.W. towards the 'so much more' that he visited this Office. (P.R.O. WORKS 14/1124)

Collingwood's desire to tackle conservation and archaeological matters upon a large scale, and his frustration with piecemeal approaches – wherein the public must be appealed to on sentimental grounds above all others – is revealed in his autobiography (Collingwood 1939, 123). Funding for the project from the Rockefeller Foundation would not have been without precedent: when the Stonehenge appeal was struggling to meet its target in 1929 John Bailey of the National Trust had suggested appealing to the Rockefeller Foundation, on the grounds that the Foundation had provided financial assistance for the conservation of Versailles (P.R.O. WORKS 14/488). Moreover, throughout the 1930s the Rockefeller Foundation supported archaeological excavation in the Middle East. Hope of a sympathetic hearing may have also been encouraged by an article written by John D. Rockefeller Jr, in 1937 in *National Geographic* in which he spoke of his ambition to see colonial Williamsburg in Virginia free 'entirely from alien or inharmonious surroundings' (in Lowenthal 1985, 326).

Whether the Wall archaeologists ever made an appeal to the Rockefeller Foundation is not known. It seems unlikely given that there is no further mention of it in the archives. However, after consultations with Sir George MacDonald and Parker Brewis (MacDonald 1940, 134), it was decided to appeal for funds to the Pilgrim Trust, already involved in funding the semi-official preservation scheme. If the funds could be raised, the plans were to extend this scheme with the backing of the 1931 Act so as to cover the area threatened by Greenhead Quarry at Walltown and to halt the threat posed to the Vallum by proposed new housing at West Denton in Northumberland. (A length of the Wall had been destroyed the previous year at West Denton.) Funds were also needed to prevent the threat of natural erosion at milecastle 49 at Harrow's Scar, following a landslip in 1936. It was promised that all of these sites would be taken into the forthcoming preservation scheme if the Pilgrim Trust would provide half of the necessary compensation.

These hopes were dashed when, on 8 February 1938, it was learnt that the Pilgrim Trust would only provide funds for the conservation of milecastle 49. The President of the Society of Antiquaries of London, Sir Frederick Kenyon, summarised the situation, as he saw it, in an anniversary address to the Society on 28 April 1938:

A few years ago it was discovered that although Hadrian's Wall might be scheduled as an ancient monument, there was nothing to prevent anybody from quarrying up to its immediate vicinity, thus destroying its amenities and also the whole of its intelligibility as a work of delimitation or defense. The then Prime Minister was genuinely shocked at this state of things, and steps were taken which were generally understood to have secured the future of this unique national monument. It was therefore no small shock to find that this protection is purely illusory. It only means that, if a particular part of the wall is threatened, His Majesty's Government will allow other people to save it at their own cost. At the present time a section of the wall, including the only part which has never been touched by restoration, is threatened by the approach of a quarry; and the official attitude appears to be that, if the work provides employment for some scores of men, then a historic monument must be sacrificed. If the public spirit of private individuals will find the means to compensate the quarry company, the Government has apparently no objection; but it shows no sign of accepting any responsibility for the matter, or indeed of taking any interest in it. We can only hope that, as so often before, private generosity may save the nation from a public scandal ... (Kenyon 1938, 233–34)

The Office of Works agreed with Sir Frederick, but the problem remained that if the 1931 Act was implemented, then it would be necessary to pay compensation at such a level as would persuade the leaseholders at Melkridge, Cawfields and Walltown to relinquish their rights to quarry in the vicinity of the Wall. Meanwhile, although Simpson reported that Colonel Joicey at Walltown was most civil, the threat of quarrying remained, more imminent even than the danger posed in 1930. Raby summarised his own view of the situation in a letter to the Treasury, dated 7 May 1938:

In 1931 Parliament gave us powers to protect the surroundings of Ancient Monuments and as you know the primary object of that Act was to get ahead with the protection of the Roman Wall. For various reasons things proceeded rather slowly but the main obstacle has always been that of finance. At the end of 1932 when we were ready to start with the scheme, Mr. Ormsby Gore who was then First Commissioner had the whole scheme put to the Treasury and the Chancellor of the Exchequer decided that there was no prospect in the financial circumstances of that time of making the money available.

Since then the scheme has been revived and we obtained semi-official approval from the Treasury to carry out a limited scheme on the assumption that we should endeavour to meet the cost without asking for any additional money on our Subhead E. In making this proposal we were imposing upon ourselves a considerable sacrifice as it could scarcely be argued that it was Parliament's intention in passing the Act not to follow it up at some future date by making adequate provision for the cost of the scheme. So many promises and assurances have been made to archaeologists that we are finding ourselves in a difficult position in view of their criticisms.

Their discontents have been brought to a head and concentrated on the Greenhead [Walltown] section of the Roman Wall. In our anxiety to limit expenditure of compensation we had merely provided in our draft scheme that quarrying here should continue only during the currency of the existing lease. At that time we expected that the Wall in this section would continue to be destroyed at the slow rate of quarrying which had been going on for many years, but as we have now explained in earlier correspondence this position is now altered and quarrying is now proceeding by a newer and more rapid manner. This will involve the destruction of an unspoiled stretch of the Wall which can only be saved if the Quarry Company move the area of destruction further east and are compensated for their additional expense.

It becomes, as you will see, simply a matter of money and archaeologists are rightly saying that there is no other country in Europe in which a Monument of this importance would be allowed to be destroyed after the lapse of so many centuries simply for the want of a comparatively small sum of money. (P.R.O. WORKS 14/1287)

In Raby's view, it was clearly imperative that Lansbury's Act should now be implemented.

Finally, at the eleventh hour, the decision was made to enforce the preservation scheme. On 20 May a total of £16,000 was agreed as compensation:

Compensation was paid by the Treasury 'with greatest reluctance' despite the approval of Parliament: £1,000 to the mineral owner and £15,000 to the company to cover the cost of realigning their plant. This was also on the understanding that they did not oppose the Preservation Scheme, which was at last published. (Charlton 2004, 5)

A preservation order was finally published, in the *London Gazette*, on 9 December 1938: the Roman Wall and Vallum Preservation Scheme covered 15 miles of the central section of the Wall (from Walwick in the east to Thirlwall Castle in the west) (P.R.O. WORKS 14/1287). (The terms of the scheme may be found in Appendix II.)

Yet, even now, the saga of prevarication continued; for the start of the war meant that the new scheme was not finally ratified. Consequently, in the summer of 1942, in response to the demand for whinstone for surfacing RAF airfields, the Walltown quarry once more began to advance towards the Wall. F. G. Simpson, assisted by John Charlton, again stepped into the breach – perhaps literally (Northumberland Record Office (A)ZBL 52/1). In February 1943 he appealed to Raby for assistance, visiting him in person at the Palace Hotel in Rhyll. This final part of the story is recollected by John Charlton:

[In] February 1943 F.G. Simpson came to Rhyll (where sections of the department [at this date called the Ministry of Works] not directly concerned with the War were now stationed) to say that a hundred yards of the Wall had been demolished at Walltown, where over 80 men were employed. There was less damage at the smaller quarry (35 men) at Cawfields, but there was a threat to the viewpoint looking towards the milecastle. (Charlton 2004, 5–6)

Raby immediately wrote to the Treasury and sent John Charlton to London to inform the Society of Antiquaries at Burlington House of the situation and to apprise Sir Eric de Normann, 'the department's formidable under-secretary' (Charlton 2004, 6). De Normann in turn sent Charlton to John Dower, at the Ministry of Housing and Local Government, and to Dr I. G. Moore, a civil engineer at Chilmark quarry in Wiltshire.

According to Charlton, John Dower

knew the Wall well, having married the eldest daughter of Sir Charles Trevelyan of Wallington and designed the Youth Hostel, Once Brewed. He was dismayed not just at the archaeological damage being done but by the threat to his proposed Northumberland National Park if we did not acquire Wake's lease at Melkridge. He was not only a magnificent moral support to us but saw that, throughout, we had the full support of his Ministry. (Charlton 2004, 6)

There was again protest in *The Times*:

Why should we weep for Rome when the most splendid Roman monument in this country, Hadrian's Wall, is daily quarried for road metal?

asked Mr G. O. Hoskins (*The Times* 27 August 1943). But, as might be expected in the midst of war, the agitation was on a smaller scale than previously. (Charlton 2004, 6). Moore worked out a plan whereby the quarry would be allowed to continue working in a southerly direction without damaging the view from the south. At a meeting attended by the local MP, by George Hicks (Secretary of the Building Trades Union) and by Eric Birley (now a lieutenant-colonel) it was announced that there would be no job losses (Charlton 2004, 6–7). In private, Eric Birley was once again moved to verse:

BALLADE (A DOUBLE REFRAIN) OF HADRIAN'S WALL

More quarries still? Must greed for gain
Prevail once more, demolishing

The Wall we've watched with might and main?
  Confound this blasted quarrying!
  Come, Ministry of Works, and bring
Relief, else all we prize will fall
  In ruin final, shattering;
Join in preserving Hadrian's Wall!

When Vandals follow in the train
  Of Commerce! All to which we cling
Must be destroyed, whate'er the pain;
  Confound this blasted quarrying!
  Let the promoters have their fling
Elsewhere (they will not need to maull
  The Roundabout, if giv'n the Swing);
Join in preserving Hadrian's Wall!

Who can assist? I rack my brain:
  The Trust? A Nuffield? Or the King
In Council? Parliament? In vain!
  Confound this blasted quarrying!
  'The Scheme will save it'? No such thing:
Its bluff is but too clear to call
  (It might with proper strengthening,
Join in preserving Hadrian's Wall).

  Envoi

Prince, it is not enough to sing
  'Confound this blasted quarrying!'
There's been too much; so let us all
  Join in preserving Hadrian's Wall.
        (Haltwhistle, April 1943)

Finally, de Normann secured the Treasury's reluctant agreement to pay such compensation as would extinguish all industrial activity within the area of the Preservation Scheme. A preservation order was issued on 17 September 1943 (P.R.O. WORKS 14/1287) and confirmed in the *London Gazette* on 21 September. According to Charlton the compensation amounted to £75,000 to the Northumberland Whinstone Company at Walltown and £3,000 to 'the Lords and Ladies of Haltwhistle', the leaseholders at Cawfields. There then only remained Frederick Wake's lease. This was finally bought out on 3 June 1944 (Charlton 2004, 8). Charlton summarises these final manoeuvres as follows:

With the Treasury agreement there were then three interlinked courses of action: stopping the present destruction; confirming the Preservation Scheme; and getting rid of the Wake concession. As soon as the Minister told de Normann to proceed, the Preservation Scheme was confirmed – on 14th September, the Preservation Order being issued four days later. At the same time Wake agreed to sell, though it was not till 3rd June, 1944 that, partly thanks to Percy Hedley FSA, Sir Hugh Blackett's agent, he formally assigned his lease to us for £6,500. (Charlton 2004, 7)

Though, sadly, not all of those who had defended the Wall in 1930 lived to see the final successful conclusion of their actions, the threat to the Wall that had persisted in one form or another since 1930 had, at last, been contained.

Yearning for Better Things

In the wake of the breakup of the Clayton estate, it is clear that the proposal to begin a new quarry at Melkridge instigated not just a purely defensive campaign but also a campaign to ensure that no such threat might ever again arise. Both aspects of the campaign were advantaged by the recent increase in visitor numbers to the Wall, thus ensuring that it was not just a small number of archaeologists who wrote to the newspapers. The positive aspect of the campaign coincided with a move to introduce national parks to Britain. It may be remembered that in his letter to Peers of 3 April 1930 Parker Brewis floated the idea that an area from Peel Crags eastwards past Housesteads might become a national park. This idea was repeated in the letter of protest from the Newcastle Antiquaries published in *The Times* on 11 April 1930. The papers in the Public Record Office show that the subject of a national park also came up in the confidential conversations between Lansbury, Parker Brewis and Wake. On 3 February 1933 Wake wrote to Parker Brewis, dropping a heavy hint that he would be willing to sell Hotbank Farm at a low figure, adding:

> You will remember that when Mr. Lansbury was over there was a suggestion that Hot Banks should be purchased as a National Park. (P.R.O. WORKS 14/1259)

Wake eventually sold Hotbank to the National Trust in 1942. Some evidence suggests that members of the public tended to regard the Wall and Vallum Preservation Scheme as something like a national park before such things were officially introduced to this country: in particular, Sir Hugh Blackett complained that following the passing of the 1931 Act, unauthorised public access to the Wall was spoiling his shooting (P.R.O. WORKS 14/1259).

Inspired by the example of the American parks, as early as 1912 the Society for the Promotion of Nature Reserves had campaigned for the introduction of similar parks to Britain (Morris 2007, 336). In the 1920s their most vociferous champion was Lord Bledisloe. Inspired by a visit to Yellowstone Park in 1925, in 1929 he wrote to the Prime Minister, Stanley Baldwin, advocating the merits of the Forest of Dean as a national park – 'for the benefit of the tired brain workers of the country who have no quiet country home to retire to as you and I have' (in Mair and Delafons 2001, 294). To this end he volunteered rights of access to his own estate in the Forest of Dean, including access to the recently excavated Roman temple at Lydney. In 1929 the Council for the Protection of Rural England and the Council for the Protection of Rural Wales (whose secretary was Crawford's friend Wilfred Kemp) asked the newly elected Labour government to consider the idea (Morris 2007, 336–7). On 9 June 1930 Lord Bledisloe wrote to George Lansbury emphasising the benefits that his scheme might bestow upon 'nerve racked people' and 'the brain weary workers in crowded urban areas (in Mair and Delafons 2001, 295). He suggested that boy scouts and girl guides be given training to enable them to conduct visitors to sites of interest within the parks. Lansbury replied on 20 June suggesting an official inquiry.

Consequently, on 26 September 1929 Ramsay MacDonald appointed an eight-member committee, led by the Minister of Agriculture Christopher Addison, to consider the feasibility of the idea. One of its members, representing the Office of Works, was the ubiquitous Frederick Raby. The committee's first witness, in November 1929, was Lord Bledisloe. Among others, the committee also heard from the archaeologist Cyril Fox, who welcomed the idea and suggested Snowdonia and the Pembrokeshire coast as candidates for 'nationalisation' (P.R.O. WORKS 16/853). Crawford too expressed his support of the idea and in a letter to Raby dated 12 October 1929 asked him to pass on his opinions to the committee. Crawford expressed his concern not just for ancient monuments but also for their surrounding environs. He suggested the Sussex Downs and part of the Marlborough Downs and the Isle of Purbeck as possible candidates, and volunteered to supply aerial photographs should the Committee require it (P.R.O. WORKS 16/853). (Crawford's proposal that the Sussex Downs should become a national park was finally implemented in 2009.) Richard Morris has plausibly suggested that Fox and Crawford may have been influenced to support national parks via contact with Wheeler who was at the time digging on Lord Bledisloe's land at Lydney Park (Morris 2007, 338). It might also be conjectured that Crawford's shift towards communist sympathies in 1930 may in part have been inspired by discussion of national parks and by frustration at conservation problems tackled at too small a scale. To be led to sympathy for the Soviet Union through the inspiration provided by American national parks would at the time have been an unusual but not impossible intellectual journey.

It was quite common at this time for senior members of the Labour Party to be interested in national parks. MacDonald praised, in particular, the national parks of Canada (Griffiths 2007, 312–13). Furthermore, within the Labour Party, there was 'considerable support for the work of the National Trust as a custodian of land in the public interest: Hugh Dalton described it as an example of "practical Socialism in action"' (Griffiths 2007, 313). Ramsay MacDonald was also an enthusiast for the work of the National Trust (Griffiths 2007, 313fn) and, as previously mentioned, Lansbury was honourable vice-president.

It is unsurprising then that the Addison report, submitted on 23 April 1931, recommended the establishment of National Parks. Subsequently, in September 1931, in the hope of influencing parliamentary opinion, the geographer Vaughan Cornish published a pamphlet proposing 'A National Park for Housesteads by Hadrian's Wall'(Crow 1995, 139). (He had already made this recommendation to the Committee the previous September (P.R.O. WORKS 16/856).)

In customary fashion, Eric Birley made clear his support in

A BALLADE OF YEARNING FOR BETTER THINGS

The growth of the towns makes the countryside shrink
Far too much for my liking; I can't but feel triste
Or indeed quite disheartened, whenever I think
Of the way Open Spaces, once Wide, have decreased
In this England of ours; and the Nation's been fleeced
Of its Heritage (didn't Lloyd George once remark
This was so?) – nought is left but a Barmecide feast ...
If Housesteads were only a National Park!

The need's so apparent, I take pen and ink
To plead for the workers – the slum-parish priest,
For the Robert on duty, the burglar in clink,
For the shop-walker, shop-keeper, tailor, modiste,
In a word, for Hoi Polloi. It's high time I ceased
Giving details, but think of the poor City clerk!
It would serve as a tonic more potent than yeast,
If Housesteads were only a National Park!

One could use it for breeding the Muskrat, or Mink,
Or a whole host of creatures from North, South and East
And West. What a sight, when they all came to drink
In Crag Lough! Then, the tamer sort might be released
For the children to play with, at times, if one greased
The custodian's palm. It would rival the Ark
Once constructed by Noah & Sons (now deceased),
If Housesteads were only a National Park!

Envoi

Princely Office of Works, may I offer a beast
For the Zoo that there's room for 'twixt Gisland and Wark?
You might run to a cage for *Vaughan Cornish*, at least,
If Housesteads were only a National Park!

(Spring 1934)

Hopes for the introduction of a national park encompassing at least part of Hadrian's Wall had been encouraged by a visit to the Wall by no less than the Prime Minister, Ramsay MacDonald (*PSAN* 5, 184) and his daughter. There seems to be very little documentation for this visit, though it occurred just over a week before the general election. (Were a current prime minister to take a weekend off from campaigning on the eve of an election and instead walk in quiet contemplation along Hadrian's Wall it is difficult to imagine that his actions would go unreported.) No doubt the Prime Minister himself fell within Lord Bledisloe's category of 'brain weary workers'. He signed the visitors' book at Chesters museum on 17 October 1931. His letter of 20 October to Mr Scott Gunn of the Newcastle Antiquaries, thanking him for his hospitality, implies that his tour of the Wall lasted two or three days – for most of which time there was thick fog.

According to Clare Griffiths, 'MacDonald regarded his rural wanderings as an escape not only from events, but from capitalism and the ills of modern society, into a world of higher values' (Griffiths 2007, 80). However, despite his own habit of walking in remote countryside, it seems that Ramsay MacDonald had ambivalent feelings about increased access to the countryside: 'I am always for opening up the country to the crowd, but to help to open the flood gates for a turgid crowd is quite another matter' (in Griffiths 2007, 96–7). On the one hand, MacDonald sincerely wished to share his pleasure in the countryside with everyone, whatever their background, but, on the other hand, he had no wish to encounter an uneducated mob.

But it was not MacDonald's nervousness that scuppered plans for national parks; it was the Depression. Addison's recommendations were made at the very depth of the slump. Yet they were not forgotten: for example, in October 1943, in an article in *Picture Post* on 'The Threat to the Great Roman Wall' (Joad 1943, 12–15) the Cambridge philosopher C. E. M. Joad looked forward to the introduction of national parks after the war. (Interestingly, the editor of the *Picture Post* at that date was a former pupil of Collingwood's, Tom Hopkinson.) The photographs attached to this article, uncredited at the time, were by Bill Brandt, since acknowledged as one of the greatest of British photographers of the time (cf. Delaney 2004). Collingwood had died in January of this year, but one imagines that Tom Hopkinson would have remembered his old teacher as he surveyed the results of Brandt's commission.

John Dower at the Ministry of Housing and Local Government was, as John Charlton mentioned, another leading advocate of national parks. Dower advocated the creation of a Northumberland National Park that would incorporate the central section of Hadrian's Wall. He set out his arguments for national parks in *The Case for National Parks in Great Britain* (1938), published with a foreword by George Trevelyan under the initiative of the Standing Committee on National Parks (founded in 1936); and, again, in the Dower Report of 1945.

These recommendations were finally put into practice in 1949 in the form of the National Parks and Access to the Countryside Act; and this ultimately led to the formation of the Northumberland National Park in 1956.

In its aim of conserving and managing not just a site of interest but an entire landscape, the Roman Wall and Vallum Preservation Scheme may clearly be seen as a forerunner of a national park. In this respect it is appropriate that the south-west and south-east corners of the Northumberland National Park coincide with the earlier boundaries of the Preservation Scheme. (In the central section, the boundary of the National Park extends further south than the boundary of the Preservation Scheme, so as to include Vindolanda.)

1.10. Crag Lough and milecastle 39. (© Bill Brandt/
Hulton Archive/Getty Images)

1.11. Crag Lough from Hotbank. (© Bill Brandt/Hulton
Archive/Getty Images)

1.12. Cawfields Quarry. (© Bill Brandt/Hulton Archive/ Getty Images)

1.13. The Wall through the wood west of Housesteads. (© Bill Brandt/Hulton Archive/Getty Images)

The Defence of the Wall

And what of the quarrymen? Their opinions have so far not been heard, but John Parker's books, with their wealth of anecdotes and photographs, preserve something of their world. His book on *Cawfields Quarry and Railway* allows us a rare glimpse of a view that must have been common around the central section of the Wall:

> I remember quarryman 'Pud' Naiden saying that there was 'miles of waall' further on so why bother about the Cawfields end. He also thought the Romans had done us a bad turn if it meant losing jobs. (Parker n.d. *Cawfields Quarry and Railway*, 52)

Yet, despite such opinions – understandable given the unemployment of the time – there are records of the archaeologists being informed of new inscriptions uncovered by quarry blasts (*PSAN* 7, 12–13). These discoveries would have provided a welcome break from routine.

Economically, it is the Wall itself that now brings revenue to the area in the form of the visitors that it attracts; and the largely unspoiled central section, with its iconic wild and windswept views, remains one of the main attractions – it is certainly the most photographed. It has even been suggested that the present-day impact of Wall tourism upon the local economy may in some ways be comparable to the impact of the original Roman garrison. However, despite the growth in visitor numbers in the 1920s and 1930s, in the pre-war period the economic benefits of tourism were rarely mentioned in the debate over the conservation of the Wall. The geographer Vaughan Cornish was one of the very few who made any reference to the economic benefits of tourism (*PSAN* 5, 183). The conservationists' stance was rather that the Wall and its surroundings were of such interest and beauty that commercial pressures should be resisted at whatever cost. And remarkably, thanks to their ambition and the goodwill of the public, and of George Lansbury and Ramsay MacDonald, in the midst of the Great Depression and in the midst of the Second World War the conservationists got their way.

Viewed from the perspective of the history of the Labour Party the episode perhaps serves to remind us of formative influences upon the party other than the ideas of Karl Marx. However, although the government was prepared to countenance direct government intervention to save Hadrian's Wall, it felt unable to initiate any direct government scheme to reduce unemployment – in the face of this problem, while the members of the government were unanimous in denouncing the iniquities of capitalism, they seemed at a loss as to how to proceed.

George Lansbury's Act was never again implemented. But although now superseded, it is worth remembering that had Lansbury's Act *not* been passed – had quarrying been allowed to continue as originally planned – then, as the campaigners of the 1930s realised, the Wall's geographical and historical context would have been lost. Without the Act, if the Wall itself *had* survived, it would have been conserved *only* in the sense that it would not have been physically destroyed.

The ambitious scope of Wall archaeology in the interwar period is well known. That the ambitious scope of Wall conservation in the same period is not so well remembered is perhaps in part due to its success. But it should be remembered that, then as now, the untamed appearance of the central section of the Wall is not something that exists without human effort.

Part II

Consolidation

Following the passing of the Ancient Monuments Act in 1931, a number of sites associated with Hadrian's Wall began to be brought under guardianship (between 1933 and 1972, thirty sites passed into the care of the state – see Appendix VI). Consequently, the Ministry of Works Ancient Monuments Department could now assemble a group of masons dedicated to consolidating and maintaining the exposed walls and buildings that had come to light during the preceding years. Most of the exposed and consolidated sections of the Wall now to be seen owe much to the labours of the team of workmen, thirty or so strong, employed by the Department.

While the overall policy for the consolidation of the Wall and its associated structures was directed from London via the Ancient Monuments Board and its Inspectors of Ancient Monuments, it was up to the foreman in charge to carry out the requested work. Although the work of consolidating some of the exposed remains of the Roman frontier had started in the early 1930s, it is perhaps not fully realised that the majority of the Wall and the associated structures of milecastles and turrets now on view to the public were uncovered and consolidated by the Ministry of Works between 1935 and the late 1970s. The work of exposing and consolidating the Roman Wall during these years can perhaps best be followed by the detailed notes and photographs of one of the Ministry's longest serving employees: it is these that form the foundation of the second part of this book.

The Man from the Ministry

In 1927 Charles Anderson was employed by the Ministry of Works to assist in the conservation of Middleham Castle (North Yorkshire). Within about three years, he had been promoted to the job of mason, working on a number of sites across the North of England. In April 1935, he was transferred to Corbridge, and in the following years he was to play a major role in the excavation and consolidation of Hadrian's Wall: for nearly four decades it was a task he carried out with dedication, enthusiasm and care. Initially, from 1935 to 1940, Anderson worked as a Ministry mason at sites that included Corbridge, Benwell temple, Heddon-on-the-Wall, Benwell vallum causeway, Denton Burn East and Winshield Crag.

Corbridge

Excavations had begun here in 1906 and continued until 1914 (Bishop, 1994). During 1910–11, the east and west granaries were partially consolidated with a mortar capping, as these buildings were to be left open for the benefit of visitors. The site came under the guardianship of the State in 1933 as a gift from Mr David Cuthbert of Beaufront Castle; and a programme of consolidation of the exposed sections of masonry was then undertaken by the Ministry of Works to preserve the monument for future generations (Bishop and Dore 1988, 1). In April 1935, Anderson arrived at Corbridge to be met by the foreman, Mr Leeming, who was in charge of site operations.

Anderson was put to work, assisted by Bill Gibbons and Foster Dixon, consolidating the granary walls and flagstone floor as well as the columns and masonry at the south end of the building. He noted that in the course of consolidating the granary, they found a lot of Roman coins that had fallen through the joints of the floor in between the sleeper walls. Work was also carried out on the fountain (where the workmen fitted metal pins to hold the joints and fractures together), the strong room and various walls within site XII. A photograph taken in 1936 shows Anderson carrying out consolidation work on the columns in front of the granaries. A mullion found in one of the sleeper walls of the east granary was fitted with metal pins and fixed back into the granary vent.

2.1. Anderson at Corbridge, 1936.

Benwell Temple

The following year (1936) saw the start of the clearance and consolidation of the temple – perhaps dedicated to the local god Antenociticus. This site had been placed under national guardianship, as a gift, in 1936. The temple, which had been discovered in 1862, was by then being used as a local tip and was overgrown with yew trees. Without any assistance, Anderson cleared the site of the accumulated rubbish, using a horse and cart, before exposing and dismantling the walls. Following the Ministry of Works approved method for consolidating the Wall sites, he washed the dismantled stones before resetting them in a cement mortar, being careful to keep this back from the front of the stones, for the joints on the face stones were pointed with lime mortar. After the lime mortar had set a little, it was sprayed with a water syringe, which cleaned the gravel and sand in the lime mortar and gave it a weathered appearance. Many years later, Hunter Davies witnessed the process and described it as follows:

> I watched the workmen as they took to pieces a large stretch of the Wall, stone by stone. Each stone was cleaned and washed, numbered with yellow chalk according to which course of the Wall it had come from, then laid out on tiers of wooden planks, exactly in the order it had come out of the Wall. When they'd created a brand new inside – a hard core of sand and cement and smallish lumps of broken stones – they then built the Wall up again, putting in the facing stones in their original order. It was like a child's game, though one which only terribly neat children would be allowed to play. (Davies 1974, 218)

The method of consolidation will be described in greater detail later, but Hunter Davies' description captures its essence.

Two replica casts of the altars were put in place, the originals now being in the Great North Museum (*RIB* 230–231). Finally, Anderson re-turfed the site and surrounded it with a boundary fence and put up iron railings between the temple and the nearby road. (The railings were subsequently dismantled and melted down as part of the war effort.)

Heddon-on-the-Wall

Anderson and two labourers, David Gibson and a local by the name of Old Tom, began exposing and consolidating the 300-metre length of Wall here in 1936, completing the work in May 1938. When they arrived the Wall was hidden under a high mound of soil and rubbish. Trees and a hedgerow ran along the top as a boundary between two fields. At the west end of the Wall was a medieval kiln, which had been exposed from at least 1879. A drawing done in the same year shows the kiln and some of the exposed facing stones on the south face of the Wall (Whitworth 2009, 13, no. 12).

The tools supplied by the Ministry consisted of picks, shovels and wheelbarrows – the cement and lime mortar being mixed by hand shovels in the farmyard west of the site and delivered to the site in wheelbarrows. Water was delivered in the same manner. Anderson recalled that he found a short section of clay bonding in the core during the consolidation – the only time he encountered it.

While work was going on at Heddon-on-the-Wall, there was also a gang of men working at Benwell on the Vallum Crossing, which had been discovered in 1932 and examined in detail the following year by the North of England Excavation Committee under Eric Birley, Parker Brewis and John Charlton (Birley et al. 1934). It was subsequently placed under guardianship in 1934. In 1938, following the completion of archaeological investigation, the Ministry of Works team (under the guidance of Anderson) moved onto the site to begin the consolidation process. They cleaned out the Vallum ditch on each side of the causeway; exposed and consolidated both the roadway leading from the fort to the causeway and the causeway walls; built a retaining wall along the north side of the site; and fixed a boundary fence. Various methods to maintain the steep sides of the vallum were tried, but none were very successful until a rough layer of stone core was layed down the vallum slopes and covered with turf. The ditch was then backfilled by 3 or 4 feet. (In 1938 Anderson ordered 2 tons of cement for the site at a cost of £4 3s 10d.)

While supervising the work at the vallum crossing, consolidation work was also being undertaken at Denton Burn, where a short stretch of the Wall was reset. Then, within a matter of months, work started at the highest point of the Wall at Winshields (1,230 feet above sea level).

Winshields

This section of Wall, around 370 metres long, had been brought under guardianship in 1937, and work was carried out between 1938 and 1940. A field wall that stood on top of the remains of the Roman Wall was dismantled by the workmen. Assisted by two Ministry labourers, Anderson built a 150-metre-long stone field boundary wall aligned with the north side of Hadrian's Wall, to milecastle 40, completing the work in November 1940. The lower courses of the new field wall were built of any facing stones that were available and completed with whinstone from the dismantled field wall (EH file no AM 10352/01). During the course of the work, the men dug a hole at Winshields so they could collect water to mix with the cement and sand. The nearby milecastle (40), excavated by Simpson in 1908 (Simpson 1976, 86–98), remains unconsolidated and buried under a covering of soil and turf.

A photograph taken in 1938 shows workmen in the process of exposing and dismantling the north face of the Wall. Further consolidation work was undertaken in 1956, and is pictured in an Anderson photograph (Winshields album).

In 1942 Anderson volunteered for military service and was attached to the headquarters of the 1st British Infantry Division. Posted to North Africa, he saw some of the ancient Roman ruins of Algeria and Tunisia before he was transferred to Italy. By May 1946 he was on his way back to the North of England and started work on the Wall again in December. Here he was to remain until he retired in March 1974.

On returning to civilian life, his first task, with the Ministry of Works based at Corbridge, was to assemble and train a team of masons and labourers for the continuing task of exposing and consolidating the remains of Rome's northern frontier. This was to be a concerted and long-term undertaking.

In October 1947, Mr R. J. Black, Superintendent of Works at York, wrote to Mr Rawson (an architect at the Department of Works):

> Further to our discussions on the site at Corstopitum Roman Station, re. getting urgent preservation work put in hand at Chester's Bridge Abutment, Vindolanda Roman Station, Sewingshields, Winshields Crag etc, the only way I can make a start on such services, is by being provided with a utility van at Corstopitum Roman Station, so as to transport labour and materials as required, the position being that these sites are at outlandish spots, and the labour just cannot be got unless you guarantee transport. The necessary labour force could be built up at Corstopitum Roman Station. I would be pleased to learn what chance there is of being provided with a van so that a start could be made in building up this labour force. (AM file 10021/01)

Consequently, in 1948 the first motor vehicle, a Ford, was provided so that staff could be transported from Corbridge to the various sites along the Wall.

2.2. New vehicle, 1948. (Anderson)

Before this time, it was necessary for the workmen to either catch a bus from Corbridge, changing at Hexham, or travel to work by bicycle. In January 1956, the first cement mixer was delivered to the team of masons; prior to this, all mortar and cement mixing was done by shovel.

The work that followed is described below, not in any strictly chronological sequence – for groups of masons were working simultaneously on a number of sites – but on a site-by-site basis, moving westwards from Planetrees (to the east of the North Tyne).

Planetrees

This is the site where, in 1801, William Hutton encountered the Wall being dismantled (Hutton, 1802).

Situated west of milecastle 26, Planetrees was taken into guardianship in 1945. When work began here in 1948, the north face was already partly exposed, so the Ministry masons and labourers excavated the south face of the 50-metre stretch of Wall. In doing so, they uncovered a junction on the south side of the Wall between the Broad Wall, to the east, and a section of Wall only 6 feet in width that was built on top of the already laid foundations for the Broad Wall. During the consolidation, it was noted that original Roman mortar was visible in the fabric on the south face, west of the reduction point – the junction between the Broad Wall and the Narrow Wall – in the area of the drain through the Wall. Anderson says that on the Narrow Wall very little work had to be carried out apart from waterproofing the topmost one or two courses. He noted that the core of the Broad Wall was of fairly big stones but that no mortar had survived within it.

Brunton

The turret (26b) had first been excavated by Clayton in 1873 (Daniels 1978, 105) and the south face of the Wall from the turret westwards, originally bonded with clay, had also been exposed by Clayton.

The masons arrived in 1948, the site having been brought under guardianship in February of that year. They began by cutting down one or two big trees on the north side and removing their roots. A reduction point between the Broad Wall and Narrow Wall, east of the turret, was uncovered and the north face of the Wall was exposed to reveal eleven courses of standing masonry. Anderson commented of the earlier work that had been carried out on the Wall, that

> when consolidation of the south face of the Wall west of the turret commenced it was discovered that three or four courses of facing stones had been re-built dry i.e. without mortar. The remaining two or three courses were still buried in their original positions. When this face was first excavated (by Clayton) the face stones were perhaps found fallen along the side of the Wall, and the masons returning them to the Wall. In this particular case the core must have been very solid because the masons found it was much easier to cut the tails of the face stones than try and remove sufficient core to allow the stones to return to the Wall in their state. Clayton used both methods. If the core was hard, he cut off the backs of the face stones, and if the core was fairly loose and small stones he would remove the core and then you will find the face stones packed in with loose dry stones down the back. (Anderson Transcript, 2).

To the east of the turret they exposed the broad foundations with the Narrow Wall on top, and it was only necessary to reset one or two courses of the Narrow Wall on top of the wing wall. Any original Roman mortar in the joints was left in place.

Anderson noted a Roman altar on the north side of the turret. The vicar of St Oswald's church, the Reverend F. G. Westgarth, visited the site and said that the altar had been removed from in front of the church to the grounds of Brunton House and then to its position on the north side of the Wall more than 100 years ago. After discussions between Mrs Selby Woods of Brunton House, Mr P. Hedley of Corbridge, Mr Charlton (the assistant Inspector of Ancient Monuments) and Ian Richmond it was agreed that it would be better to have it returned to the church (EH file AM 10348/01). The necessary permission was obtained and the altar (*CSIR* 1988, no. 279) is now in the nave of the church. A drawing made in 1879 of the north face of the Wall at Brunton by James Irwin Coates (Whitworth 2009, 17, no. 31) shows two altars on the north side of the Wall, the larger of which is presumably the one noted by Anderson.

Chesters Bridge Abutment

The first excavations at this site had been carried out between 1860 and 1864; at the same time, a number of colour drawings were made, by David Mossman and H. B. Richardson (Bidwell and Holbrook 1989, 3, plates 1–5).

The east abutment of the bridge was given to the nation in 1946 by the owner of the Chesters estate, Captain A. M. Keith, and subsequently placed under guardianship. In the same year, F. G. Simpson carried out a small excavation of part of the landward side of the abutment on behalf of the Ministry of Works (Simpson 1976, 44–9); but it was not until 1955 that the short section of the Wall running westwards down to the bridge foundations, together with the tower and water mill race, was finally consolidated. In the mid-1960s the barrel-shaped stone located during earlier excavations (probably a balance-weight) was broken by a party of visitors from Newcastle University. It was repaired by Ministry staff.

Chesters Fort

Once the site had been placed under guardianship in 1954, the Ministry's team of masons and labourers began the work of consolidation. The fort walls and gateways as well as the Headquarters building, the Commandant's House and the barrack buildings were consolidated, as was the short length of Wall on the east side of the fort. Prior to consolidating the bathhouse, excavated in 1884–85, a selective excavation of the entire complex was undertaken in 1957–58 by J. P. Gillam. During the course of consolidation, the masons uncovered a short length of Roman lead piping leading from the earlier cold bath together with a number of T-shaped metal brackets fastening thin stone slabs to the hot room (*caldarium*) walls.

When the strong room in the Headquarters building was being cleared out prior to consolidation in 1956, a dedicatory slab of the 1st Cohort of Dalmatians was found (Coulston and Philips 1998, no. 237) which is now on display in the museum at Chesters fort. There are 160 photographs taken by Anderson in the Chesters album showing the site prior to, during and after consolidation. Work continued until 1960.

Black Carts

A discussion in the House of Commons in April 1958 referred to

> the section running through the field belonging to Black Carts farm – a
> section which is overgrown with bushes and quite sturdy trees, the roots of
> which are eating into the core. Before many years pass the facing stones will
> be forced apart and that particularly fine section of Wall will be lost forever.
> (*Hansard* 2 April 1958, 1345).

The site of Black Carts, brought under guardianship in 1970, was in 1958
covered with a line of trees and scrub. However some of the south face of
the Wall and the turret (29a) had been exposed by John Clayton in 1873 so
as to allow passing visitors a glimpse of the facing stones. Interestingly, in
retirement, in a comment made to the Inspector of Ancient Monuments on
14 February 1980, Anderson says he thought of himself as the 'unofficial
custodian' of the site as he found himself visiting the site many times and
replacing stones which had fallen from either the turret or the Wall face.

After removing the trees and vegetation, the masons exposed and
consolidated the north face of the Wall as well as the turret. A series of
photographs taken by Mr Anderson shows the Wall as left by Clayton, the
consolidation in progress, and finally the finished work. Anderson, in a taped
commentary on the photographs he took of this section, observed:

> I think Clayton must have been a very thoughtful fellow; he also appears to
> have the public in mind, or visitors to the Wall. When he exposed any Wall
> section, it was always an easy section to reach.

He took a couple of photographs to show the difference between Clayton's
core packing and the Roman core and to show how the Roman core work
and lime mortar was built in layers, each one binding and strengthening the
Wall. He noted that there were

> no chamfered stones at Black Carts but what we did find in position were
> three centurial stones [Charlesworth 1973, 97]; one on the south face west
> of the turret, on the lower courses, and two in position on the north face,
> which is supposed to be unusual, as an expert told us they were only found
> on the south face.

Another centurial stone was found fallen on the north side of the Wall
82 metres west of the turret. It referred, for the first time in Britain, to
the rank of *princeps primus* (*Britannia* 1972, 354, 12). Before the turret
was consolidated, a re-excavation was carried out in 1971 by Dorothy

2.3. Black Carts Turret (29a), during restoration. (Anderson)

Charlesworth (1973a). Quantities of facing stones with possible quarry batch marks on them have recently been located in the Black Carts section of Wall (*Britannia* 1989, 333).

Carrawburgh Temple

The temple to Mithras, discovered in 1949, was excavated by Professor Richmond and J. P. Gillam in 1950 (Richmond and Gillam 1951). After it was taken into guardianship in 1953, the Ministry masons consolidated the structural remains for public viewing. Anderson recalled:

> This was an interesting little monument. I made the imitation concrete posts and altars inside the temple. They must have been fairly good as the visitors started to break pieces off. They thought it was proper stone, fossil timber at least.

Anderson made a number of models of the temple from a mould. Professor Richmond and John Gillam both possessed one of these models; and a photograph of one of the models appeared in Anderson's unpublished memoir, *In the Footsteps of the Romans*. In 1957, when the workmen were landscaping

2.4. Shrine to the Nymphs, Carrawburgh, 1960. (Anderson)

the ground around the temple, they uncovered an altar dedicated to the *Nymphs* and the *Genius Loci* (*RIB* 3316). It was recorded that Anderson gave his enthusiastic co-operation to the latter excavation.

Sewingshields

This 2-mile length of Wall runs from turret 33b to turret 35b and was brought under guardianship in 1946. Coesike turret (33b), discovered in 1913 by F. G. Simpson, was examined in the same year, and again in 1947, and completely excavated in 1970 (Miket and Maxfield 1972). During consolidation the Ministry masons located two inscriptions, one within the blocking of the internal recess and another in the north face of the Wall (*Britannia* 1971, 291, 10–11).

West Grindon turret (34a), also discovered by Simpson in 1913, was excavated in 1971 (Charlesworth 1973) and then consolidated by the Ministry of Works. However, the central section of Wall at Sewingshield Crags began to be exposed and consolidated already in 1958. Sewingshields turret (35a) was excavated in 1958 on the behalf of Durham University Excavation Committee (Woodfield 1965, 151) and was consolidated at the same time as the curtain

Wall was being uncovered by the Ancient Monuments team led by Anderson. Anderson recalled:

> When operations commenced at Sewingshields there was no exposed Wall to be seen at any point. I had a word with Mr. Rawson, the architect at the time, and suggested that we just expose any short section existing with face stones for the benefit of hikers. This he agreed to do. I had no trouble with the management in those days, they would usually ask me where I was going next or how did I know it was Roman. So what I did first was put down a few trial trenches in at points where I thought we might find a nice piece of Wall, where the mounds or high mounds were on the ground, or slacks on the hillside. With our luck we found a few reasonably nice pieces of Wall. This was carried out just from the milecastle area, west of the farm, to the point on the crags overlooking the lake. The trenches were made in 1958. This was a site where we discovered a lot of original mortar. At the time it was fairly sound and it was decided to retain as much as possible. This we did, but it was a mistake. The first frost that comes along soon destroys it.

After excavating and consolidating the best surviving sections along the top of Sewingshields Crags, a number of trial trenches were dug along the line of the field wall down to the extreme west boundary of Sewingshields Farm. The results were not encouraging and no further sections of Wall were exposed at the west end. Anderson noted a variation in the core composition where there was a reduction point. He commented that where the Wall was narrower, the core was also narrower than in the wider sections of Wall, and the original mortar was very hard.

The then farmer at Sewingshields, Mr Tulley, told Anderson that there were three or four centurial stones north of the Wall, in the field somewhere beyond his farm. Unfortunately Anderson was never shown their precise location and they appear never to have been recovered. A stone burial cist (containing the skeleton of a male) was uncovered on Sewingshields Crags on the south side of the Wall, west of Sewingshields woods, during excavations carried out in 1976–77, and was consolidated *in situ* by the masons (Breeze 2006, 228).

2.5. Sewingshields, original Roman core (1). (Anderson)

2.6. Sewingshields, original Roman core (2). (Anderson)

2.7. Sewingshields, south face. (Anderson)

2.8. Wall at west end of Sewingshields. (Anderson)

Housesteads

Housesteads fort, which as we have seen was given to the National Trust in 1930 by Jack Clayton, was taken into the care and guardianship of the Ministry of Works in 1951, as it was felt that this body had greater expertise in the management of archaeological sites (Woodside 1995, 67). Excavations have been carried out within the fort since 1822, and consolidation of the remains was deemed necessary in order to prevent their deterioration. As secretary of the local committee of the National Trust, Eric Birley was closely involved with the excavation and maintenance of the exposed walls. At a meeting at Housesteads in March 1949 between Mr O'Neill (Chief Inspector of Ancient Monuments) and Mr Wright (architect to the Ministry of Works) and National Trust representatives (including George Howard, C. H. D. Acland and, as the local NT committee secretary, Eric Birley), it became apparent that disagreements existed regarding the treatment of the walls of the fort and buildings. Mr Howard recorded that Mr O'Neill had described the National Trust view as reactionary and had hoped that their view was one 'which had long been forgotten'; and he vehemently rejected the word 'restoration' as applied to the Ministry of Works methods. Eric Birley is noted as saying 'that the archaeological and instructional aspect of Housesteads should be paramount and that its historic interest can best be forwarded by treating it as the Ministry of Works have treated Chesterholm (Vindolanda) since he put it under their guardianship'. He went on to say that if the NT did not adopt the Ministry methods, he would regretfully have to resign as secretary of the local committee in order to be free to attack the Trust through the learned societies and by every means in his power. Howard continues in his report:

> Mr O'Neill seemed concerned only to protect the reputation of the Ministry of Works and to get Housesteads under its guardianship. He did not hesitate to use the threat of compulsory acquisition if our [NT] methods did not meet with the Ministry's approval. The committee are asked to decide whether to preserve the atmosphere at Housesteads – or take the drastic and irretrievable step of handing it over to the Ministry of Works and having it reduced to the same soulless level as the rest of the Wall which is under their tidy guardianship.

On 18 May 1949, Birley wrote to the National Trust Area Agent C. H. D. Acland regarding the west wall of Housesteads fort north of the west gate: 'I wonder whether it might not be possible to ask the Inspectorate of Ancient Monuments whether the Ministry of Works staff could be made available to do the job? Anderson, their charge-hand at Corbridge, is a first class man, and we need have no anxiety at all if the job could be done by him and some of his men.'

2.9. Housesteads latrines (1). (Anderson)

2.10. Housesteads latrines (2). (Anderson)

2.11. Housesteads latrines (3). (Anderson)

After further negotiations, a compromise was agreed between the National Trust and the Ministry of Works whereby the fort and its associated buildings would be given the Ministry-approved consolidation, and the National Trust sections of Wall westwards to Hotbank would follow the 'turf topped' method.

The method of consolidation (previously described) was that which the Ministry of Works carried out on all of the ancient monuments in its care and guardianship and which had the approval of the Ancient Monuments Board for England as well as that of the many respected and eminent Wall archaeologists. Eventually, all of the fort walls, gates and towers as well as the Headquarters building, the Commandant's house, granaries, latrines, hospital and the civilian buildings to the south of the fort were consolidated. In July 1953, Professor Ian Richmond wrote to the National Trust in London regarding the portion of Wall for which it was responsible between Housesteads and Crag Lough:

I do not know whether your officials have seen the work recently executed by the Ministry at the west gate, the northwest angle-tower and the north granary at Housesteads. I believe they would join me in praising what they saw and accept the wise policy followed by the Trust in that case [i.e. the adoption of the Ministry method].

In April 1954 Mr Acland, NT Area Agent, wrote to the Ministry Superintendent of Works at York and admitted: 'I was most impressed with the work you have done at Housesteads, especially the turret at the N.W.' The work had been carried out by Ministry masons under the guidance of Charles Anderson.

The three Anderson photograph albums of Housesteads show the sections of the fort walls and buildings prior to, during, and after consolidation. Anderson also took a number of photographs at the start of excavations in the Commandant's House in 1967 undertaken by Dorothy Charlesworth of the Ancient Monuments Department.

In 1963, when the latrines, which had been excavated in 1898 and then backfilled, were opened up and prepared for consolidation, Anderson took photographs of the work in progress. Between 1967 and 1973 a number of further excavations were undertaken within the confines of the fort. Again, it was Anderson who oversaw the consolidation work.

Vindolanda

The fort of Vindolanda, but not the *vicus*, was placed under guardianship in 1939 by Eric Birley. The fort walls, gates and Headquarters building were consolidated prior to 1945. In 1970 the bathhouse was excavated by Robin Birley of the Vindolanda Trust and then consolidated by the Ministry team under the supervision of Anderson, the work being completed by 1972. When Anderson retired from the Department of the Environment, he was appointed as Consultant for Consolidation by the Vindolanda Trust and in that capacity gave invaluable advice during the consolidation of the *vicus* between 1974 and 1976.

Hotbank

The Hotbank sector of Wall had come into the ownership of the National Trust in 1942. By 1960 the Ministry and the National Trust were beginning to co-operate on the question of the methods of consolidation to be used on those parts of the Wall which belonged to the Trust. This co-operation followed from a meeting between the two organisations that had taken place in London on 10 October 1957. In November 1960, Anderson wrote to the Superintendent of Works based in York to say that work on the above section was completed and that 18 yards of Wall had been consolidated. Four or five courses of dry wall had been removed from the top of the Roman Wall, which had then been secured. The core had been rebuilt and lime pointed as well as the facing stones in the Roman wall. The dry wall was rebuilt above the Roman Wall and turf laid on the top of the Wall. Anderson supplied a sketch

2.12. Hotbank, original Roman core and Wall with Clayton rebuild removed. (Anderson)

of a cross-section of the Wall showing the original Roman Wall with the later dry wall and turf capping on top. The National Trust supplied one mason as well as a part-time labourer, an old-age pensioner. The final cost of this work was £255 16s 10d, which was paid by the National Trust.

Castle Nick (Milecastle 39)

In August 1957 Mr Acland (Area Agent for the National Trust) wrote an internal memo informing those concerned of a plan to carry out an experiment on six sections of Wall east of Castle Nick to try to solidify the original Roman mortar by impregnating it with a solution of silica. This was discussed at a meeting in London between the National Trust (Lord Esher, Hon. Nicolas Ridley, Mr Romilly Fedden and Mr Acland), the Ancient Monuments Board (Sir Mortimer Wheeler, Mr Ralegh Radford and Professor Ian Richmond) and the Ministry of Works (Mr Baillie Reynolds, Mr Gilyard-Beer, Mr Rawson and Mr Lewis). After discussing the proposed work at Hotbank Crag it was agreed that the applications of silicones and silicates would not be undertaken on the Wall east of Castle Nick – Acland's proposal was dropped.

In 1968 the Ministry masons consolidated 112 feet of Wall at the west end of Castle Nick at a cost of £220 – an instance of co-operation between the Ministry of Works and the National Trust. They carried out first-aid treatment to a further 330 feet by cleaning out and lime pointing cavities at a cost of £100 (National Trust File HW\EG 1969–73).

This co-operation continued when, at a meeting in September 1968 between the National Trust, the Ministry of Works and the Ancient Monuments Board it was recommended that a joint operation on two sections of the Wall would take place in 1969 – at the exposed core work immediately east of Castle Nick and on a section of original Roman footings west of Housesteads milecastle 37. It was decided that the Ministry would provide one man for the operation and that the National Trust would provide an assistant who would learn from him. The Ministry quote for the cost of the work was £320.

Starting on 2 June, the length of Wall belonging to the National Trust to the east of Castle Nick received the attentions of the man from the Ministry assisted by the National Trust mason. According to Anderson: '[They] thought he would know all about consolidation of the Roman Wall when he had completed a short section, I don't think he has recovered from the shock yet.' Within the core was very hard original Roman mortar that was exposed. Anderson recalled that someone from the National Trust erected a sign saying 'Original Roman Mortar'. This was quickly removed when it was realised how well it functioned as an advertisement to souvenir hunters.

2.13. Original Roman core, east of milecastle 39. (Anderson)

Cawfields

The Cawfields section of the Wall includes two turrets (41a, 41b) and a milecastle (42). The milecastle was exposed by Clayton in 1847–48 and the turrets located in 1912 by F. G. Simpson (Simpson 1976, 108). Consolidation work first began here in 1960, the year it came under guardianship, and it continued through to 1973. Anderson noted that the milecastle had 'become mostly covered again with soil and turf' and that the south face of the Wall had also been exposed, perhaps at the same time as the milecastle, from the gate into the field (west of the milecastle) as far as Thorny Doors. He said that there were a few courses of original or undisturbed face work.

> I lime pointed the face joints of the original work, but Clayton work I left 'angry' with outline pointing. The north face of the Wall was covered with soil and shrubbery and well hidden from view with the exception of the top course or so in the milecastle area. To the east of Thorny Doors the Wall was below ground level and for the majority of the distance there was a dry stone wall built along top.

Part of the dry stone wall was dismantled and rebuilt about 30 metres south of the Wall (and turret 41a) and parallel to it to form a new field boundary for the benefit of the farmer. Speaking in 1980, Anderson recalled visiting the Wall with Mr Gilyard-Beer, the Inspector of Ancient Monuments, and

> seeing the National Trust excavating along the north side of the Wall at the same time re-building the face with the stones they were uncovering – Clayton all over again. Mr. GB soon put a stop to that … unless of course they have made a move in the last year or two, like the vallum mound in the car park at Twice Brewed, which was frozen for many years, but has disappeared in the last year or two.

In a note dated 1 March 1967, Anderson reported that the owner of Twice Brewed had removed a further 20 yards of turf from the south side of the south mound of the vallum. In 1962 the Inspector of Ancient Monuments, Mr Gilyard-Beer, had ruled that they must not consolidate any masonry unless they were certain that it was Roman. It was also suggested that from Cawfields milecastle (42) westwards to the field gate – unless the masons were certain that the original Roman work went higher – the wall should be reduced in height to three or four courses at most. The reduction work was not to be done in a single operation, as it would attract attention, but by working on different areas every few days as inconspicuously as possible. This does not seem to have been carried out to judge from the height of the Wall as now consolidated.

Anderson was well aware that Clayton and others had been working on the Wall before him, repairing and rebuilding, and he could tell where the earlier interventions had occurred:

> Clayton made a good job of his coursing. If you get any alterations, anyone else following, the farmer or anyone else like that, the courses were not so good. They'd be up and down, little pieces of stone packed in here and there to level up the courses. Clayton was very particular with his coursing of masonry. That's one way you can tell Clayton from the rest of the world.

Anderson was aware that, where there was grass growing in the Wall joints, it was likely to be undisturbed Roman material. He kept the Inspector of Ancient Monuments, Dorothy Charlesworth, who had taken over from Gilyard-Beer, informed of anything out of the ordinary that he found on the Wall, including the unusually large blocks in the north face of the Wall just east of milecastle 42 (Charlesworth 1963) and three possible parapet stones found in the fallen debris (Charlesworth 1968 69–74).

At the east end of Cawfields, he commented on the exceptionally hard Roman mortar that came right up to the face joints, indicating that there had been later repairs or rebuilding of the Wall in this area, probably during the Severan period (Rushworth and Barker 1997, 10).

Anderson also expressed an opinion regarding the different reduction points along the length of the Wall based on his observations of the type of core material and the width of the Wall. He tells us that he checked the foundations and the few courses at the bottom of the Wall where the reductions occurred and these he found to be original. He noted that the Wall narrowed between the reduction points and then widened out to its normal thickness. He suggests that the narrow sections were where the Wall had been left open while it was being built to allow access to the north side. This access point was then closed up when the section of Wall was finished, for he noted that the core at the reduction point (especially at Sewingshields) was 'just a load of old rubbish they had picked up from anywhere'. It is interesting to note that a photograph in the Walltown album shows that the masons had left a small section of Wall covered with soil while they were consolidating the section on either side, so that they had access to a large water tank on the north side and also to allow a wheeled vehicle or dumper truck to cross the Wall without damaging the remains. Anderson was aware of the Wall builders' need for adequate drainage along the Wall. He noted that a dip in the line of the Wall was a potential water collecting point but that it never used to stand there.

> There was an opening through below the Wall. Whether the Romans were aware of this and they didn't put in a drain – but the water got away all right. Sometimes you get fractures in the rock which are better than drains.

At Thorny Doors, the masons exposed one of the highest sections of surviving original Wall, standing 10 feet high (see Fig. 2.17). According to Anderson:

> It's an excellent state of preservation of this piece for height. I think it has been saved by the fact that all the rock and so on had washed down the hillside and covered this little piece close to the crag side.

Anderson noted the difference in weathering on the facing stones between the worn blocks in the top section and those in the lower courses that had hardly been weathered at all. The facing stones at Thorny Doors showed the greatest amount of weathering that he had seen anywhere along the Wall. He thought this was because the gap in the hillside acted like a flue.

> The wind and storms would be blowing from the north very fiercely and nothing weathers the stone more than the wind and rain. You can see all the edges of the stone worn away especially the top half. The bottom half must have been pretty well covered in Roman times, because there is hardly any weathering at all on the lower few courses. I haven't seen stone weathered so much on the Roman Wall anywhere as they are at Thorny Doors.

He also pointed out, in a couple of the photographs taken at Thorny Doors, possible Roman putlog holes in the Wall face, for scaffolding poles. Certainly, during the consolidation process, the workmen had to use scaffolding due to the height of the Wall. He said that at the extreme west end of Cawfields there was also a lot of very hard mortar but the frost got to it and it could not be saved from disintegration.

2.14. Cawfields Quarry and Ministry of Works van. (Anderson)

2.15. Cawfields, north face, looking east. (Anderson)

2.16. Cawfields, Thorny Doors, north face (1). (Anderson)

2.17. Cawfields,
Thorny Doors, north face
(2). (Anderson)

2.18. Cawfields, milecastle 42, being uncovered and consolidated. (Anderson)

Great Chesters

Parts of the site had been opened up as early as 1894 (Gibson 1903, 19–64) and although the site has never been taken into guardianship it was felt necessary that there should be some remedial work undertaken. First-aid treatment was carried out at Great Chesters on the various walls of the fort, including the West gate, the barracks and the bathhouse. A modern mortar pointing was applied between the exposed joints to protect the upstanding masonry from further frost and stock damage. In 1969 the repairs to the stonework of the strong room, including replacing and re-bedding loose and fallen stone, was estimated at £200. Work started on 2 June of that year and was completed on 24 July at a final cost of £189 17s 9d.

2.19. Great Chesters, 1958. (Anderson)

Walltown

A total of 400 metres of Wall were brought under guardianship by a deed of gift in 1939; and, as previously mentioned, operations at Walltown quarry finally ceased in 1943. Turret 45a, which had been discovered in 1883 by Clayton's chief excavator, Mr W. Tailford, was examined in 1959 prior to consolidation (Woodfield 1965, 162). Turret 45b had also been discovered in 1883 and was destroyed by quarrying activity soon afterwards, as predicted by Collingwood Bruce (1883, 235). The consolidation of Walltown began in 1959 and continued into the early 1960s. After it was excavated and exposed – and prior to and during its consolidation – Anderson took a number of photographs of turret 45a. They show that the turret had been built directly on top of the underlying bedrock. During the consolidation of the Wall the adjacent ground surface was landscaped.

> On the north side we usually took a levelling straight out to the cliff face which is never very far away and on the south side we took a level or line from the bottom offset course out into the field as long as it was good to look at and suited the eye.

Of all of the sections of Wall that Anderson helped expose, his favourite was at Walltown Crags:

> Walltown is one of the best and most interesting of all the sections of the Wall I have had the pleasure to expose. There had been no modern interference; Clayton worked in the area, but for a change he failed to leave his trademark. All the curtain Wall we exposed was original and in an excellent state of preservation and in most cases, it was only necessary to remove the top course or two and the top layer of core for re-setting and waterproofing, and the remainder of the face joints were raked out, removing soil and perished mortar, washing out with water and re-pointed with new lime mortar.

When this section of Wall was exposed, Anderson was impressed with the quality and class of building work that had survived, standing up to fourteen courses high. He also noted that the original builders had constructed the Wall directly on top of the natural bedrock without the normal foundations found in other sections of the Wall. He photographed a section of the core that had been buttressed as the Wall climbed the steep incline of the slope. Several drains run through the Wall in this section and the north side of one of these has a curved top stone.

Anderson noted that beneath the collapsed Roman stonework from the face of the Wall there was a certain amount of soil build-up, which must have happened prior to any Wall collapse. He also observed that the chamfered

2.20. Walltown, prior to consolidation, 1959. (Anderson)

2.21. Walltown, south face, west of turret 45a, during excavation and consolidation. (Anderson)

2.22. Walltown, south face, 1960. (Anderson)

2.23. Walltown, surviving Wall and tumble. (Anderson)

2.24. Walltown, Wall face and chamfered stone. (Anderson)

2.25. Walltown, south face, west of turret 45a. (Anderson)

2.26. Charles Anderson
at Walltown.

stones, which are shown in a large pile in one of the photographs, must have
come from the top of the Wall and that they were mainly, but not exclusively,
found on the north side of the Wall. He noted that the original Roman mortar
was in a bad state and they did not find any that they could do anything
with. Photographs of this section of Wall show how much of it was visible
prior to work commencing. Numerous other photographs depict the work of
uncovering and consolidating the Wall. At least eleven centurial stones were
found in the material fallen from the Wall, as well as one *in situ* built upside
down into the north face of the Wall. Their locations are noted in the *Journal
of Roman Studies* for 1960, 1961 and 1962. In 1969 Anderson delivered
fourteen inscribed facing stones to the Museum of Antiquities in Newcastle.
Twelve were from Walltown and two from Sewingshields. Professor Eric Birley
commented that the find spots had been noted with exemplary exactness by
Mr Charles Anderson, the Ministry's charge hand, and that they will give
considerable help in working out the exact lengths built by individual centuries
(Birley 1961, 258).

Long Byre

This is a short stretch of Wall on the west side of the road leading from Greenhead to Gilsland. Anderson recalled that in 1957:

> some road work was going on near this section one day as I passed, the foreman in charge gave me permission to check if there could be any Wall. I was lucky it was passed on to the excavators, after which we carried out our treatment.

It seems that he must have then informed Mr J. P. Gillam, who reported the fact to the Inspectorate of Ancient Monuments, which then arranged for an emergency excavation to be carried out, in July 1957, under the direction of Peter Salway. On completion of the excavation, the Ministry of Works consolidated 8 metres of the Wall. If it had not been for Anderson's observation, this section of Wall might have been lost in the road-widening scheme.

Poltross Burn

Milecastle 48 at Poltross Burn came under guardianship in 1938, having been first excavated in 1886 and again in 1909–10 (Gibson and Simpson 1911). In 1960 the railway cutting close to the milecastle was filled with ballast, the increased rail traffic having made the shoring unsafe. The Ministry of Works reopened the site in 1965–66 and carried out their usual consolidation treatment of the whole site. At the east end of the Wall, a reinforced concrete beam was placed below the ground surface, adjacent to the foundations, to stop the Wall from sliding down the slope into the Poltross Burn.

Gilsland Vicarage

The south face of the Wall had been cleared of soil in 1894 by Haverfield – but a short piece of the Wall had been cleared already in June 1877 by the Reverend A. Wright, vicar of Gilsland, during an excursion of the Cumberland and Westmorland Antiquarian and Archaeological Society. The section of Wall through the garden of Gilsland Vicarage was placed under guardianship in 1945. In 1949 Anderson and the Ministry team began clearing the soil from the top and sides of the Wall, as well as dismantling the field wall built on top. More than 200 metres of the Wall was thus exposed for consolidation. While Anderson was working there, the vicarage was purchased by a local building contractor who told him he was going to carry out some alterations. There were several centurial stones around the front door (Collingwood 1933, 168)

2.27. Poltross Burn, milecastle 48, 1965. (Anderson)

and Anderson was told he could take them, otherwise they would be used in the rebuilding. He removed them to the fort at Corbridge. These must be *RIB* 1856, 1857, and possibly 1858.

Willowford and Milvain

The Willowford bridge abutment came under guardianship in 1939 with the rest of the Wall eastwards (Willowford Farm and Milvain) coming under guardianship in 1946. Work on the length of Wall from the main road to Willowford bridge was carried out in three stages over a number of years. The dates for the work given by Anderson on the back of one of the photographs (Willowford, Book 2, no. 179) are: sector one (east), from the main road to where the farm track crosses the Wall, 1950–1952; sector two (central), from that point to Willowford Farm, June 1960 – June 1963; and sector three (west), from the farm to the Roman bridge abutment by the river Irthing, October 1962 – September 1964. However, some of the photographs show that work was being carried out on the eastern sector up until 1954.

Within the east section of Wall is turret 48a, which had been excavated in 1923 and then backfilled (Shaw 1926, 437–50). In an Anderson photograph taken in 1954 the south wall of the turret is visible in the wheel ruts of the old cart road leading to the farm, with a field wall on top of the Roman Wall. The old cart road was removed and a new road laid out by the men from the Ministry, the line of which is shown on one of the photographs.

In 1952 Anderson wrote to the Superintendent of Work (EH file AM 10048/01) saying he had put a few trenches along the line of the Wall towards Willowford and found the Wall with ten courses of ashlar and standing in several places 8 or 9 feet high, and there was any amount of stone along the side of the Wall to raise it another course or two.

In 1955 several masons opened up a section of the Wall in the central sector at Willowford so that a Ministry of Works photographer, Mr Broadrim, could make a record of their work for an exhibition held in London. These photographs are reproduced in Whitworth (1994, 69).

By 1960 works had progressed to the central sector, including turret 48b, where the Wall was uncovered from Willowford Farm eastwards towards the farm track crossing. The tree growth was removed, and although Anderson notes that there were a lot of trees to cut down, their roots did not penetrate the Wall to any great extent as they tended to extend over the sides of the monument, thus more or less holding it together. As the Wall was being opened up, by pick and shovel, the soil and rubble lying next to and covering the Wall was moved by small front-loading dump trucks and scattered around the farm fields. In parts, there were more than seven courses of original Roman facing stones *in situ*. Anderson noted the three offset courses at the bottom of the Wall on the north face and the 2 inches offset above and he related this to the Broad Wall foundations.

> This Broad Wall business puzzles me. You get three or four courses of masonry on the south face running along on the Broad foundation and then the Romans have built their Narrow Wall leaving these courses standing. I think if I'd been building the Roman Wall and changed my mind, I'd have used those stones instead of leaving them like that. Whether the mortar was too hard to remove them or whether they were used for some building purposes, it's a bit puzzling this Broad foundation business.

The central section provided a very good example of how the Wall was constructed in this part of the Wall: a course of facing stones was put in place that was then filled in with core from face to face and then a spread of lime mortar was placed on the top. This was repeated, course after course, until the desired height was reached (Willowford/Harrow's Scar, Bk 1, 100–102). One of the photographs is a close up of several courses of stonework showing original Roman mortar spread over the face of the blocks (Willowford/Harrow's Scar, Bk 1, 106). The core here was in an excellent state and is probably evidence of Severan rebuilding.

We cleaned it off, brushed it and washed it down but it didn't last very long when the frost came along. Apart from the section where the excellent core was, we found very little lime mortar worth bothering about.

Anderson was also puzzled by the size of some of the blocks in the Wall. He noted that when excavating at Willowford east (sector one), where there were two or three courses of original masonry, they found a lot of fallen stones that were much larger than those which were actually in the Wall. These larger blocks were possibly part of the superstructure of turret 48a.

At the west end of the Willowford section, from the farm to the bridge abutment, a line of mature oak trees was growing on top of the Wall and a field wall had been constructed with reused facing stones. Anderson said this was the worst section for trees. Once the trees had been felled, the removal of the stumps required the use of heavy machinery on the site, so a bulldozer, supplied by Browns of Thursby, was used to ease the root remains free of the Wall and to move the tree trunks away from the Wall face. This was the only time that such a large piece of equipment was used by the workmen along the Wall.

The bridge abutment at Willowford had been examined by Dr R. C. Shaw in 1923 and had been given to the nation in 1939 by Lord and Lady Henley, whereupon the Ministry of Works began to restore the visible remains (Simpson 1976, 49). Mr Anderson recalled that the consolidation of Willowford:

was quite straightforward, there wasn't many snags. A lot of hard work and we hadn't much interference from these so called, you know ... as you get around. They seemed to be holding you back more than allowing you to go. We had a free hand. I could just carry on with the work, and everything went nice and smoothly. We just opened the Wall out as we went, preserved it as we went, and I think it turned out to be an excellent section.

The reference to being held back probably refers to the visits by the Inspector of Ancient Monuments and the Superintendent of Works. (Doubtless the Roman masons sometimes felt the same way.) During the course of excavation and consolidation of this length of Wall, a number of centurial stones were recovered from fallen material, and photographed and recorded (see Appendix V).

At the river crossing, the Ministry of Works constructed a temporary footbridge across the Irthing so that the members of the Roman Wall Pilgrimage in 1959 and 1969 could cross from Harrow's Scar to Willowford. The cost of erecting the temporary 100-foot bridge for the 1969 Pilgrimage was £170.

2.28. Willowford, being uncovered. (Anderson)

2.29. Willowford, trees on the Wall. (Anderson)

2.30. Willowford, original Roman core. (Anderson)

2.31. Willowford, height of surviving Wall face. (Anderson)

2.32. Willowford, north face being uncovered. (Anderson)

2.33. Willowford, north face, west of farm, being uncovered. (Anderson)

2.34. Willowford, turret 45a, after consolidation. (Anderson)

2.35. Willowford, south face being uncovered. (Anderson)

2.36. Willowford, west of farm, tree felling on the Wall. (Anderson)

2.37. Willowford, west of farm, prior to consolidation (1962–64). (Anderson)

2.38. Willowford East, turret 48a showing under farm road. (Anderson)

2.39. Willowford East, prior to consolidation. (Anderson)

Birdoswald and Harrow's Scar

The 400-metre section of Wall from milecastle 49 to turret 49b, including the walls and gates of the fort, had been brought under guardianship in 1946. Anderson had been introduced to Birdoswald by the veteran Wall archaeologist F. G. Simpson. Starting work on the fort in 1948, Anderson took a number of photographs of consolidation work being carried out on the east gate. Several of these photographs show a farm building (used by the farmer, Mr Hall, to house a pack of foxhounds) outside the east wall of the fort and north of the gateway, and a field wall across the gate portals – both of which were removed by the workmen. During this time, Anderson discovered the interval towers north of the main gates on the west and east walls of the fort and also the northwest angle tower. As he recalled:

> [After] I'd been working some time I traced the inside face of the wall almost round its northern half exposing two interval towers and the north west angle tower. A man from the Ministry came along and told me it wasn't part of the Wall, the towers, and we should not have exposed them. I suppose it would be one way of clearing himself in case anything developed, but I might say the owner and the agent at the time were very interested with what we were doing.

In May 1949, in the course of removing part of the rampart backing of the east wall of the fort, north of the east gate, the Ministry workmen found a Roman bronze wrist-purse (Richmond 1951). It was conserved by the British Museum laboratory and found to contain 28 *denarii* ranging in date from 125 BC to AD 119. After the inquest, the owner, Lord Henley, presented the finds to Tullie House Museum in Carlisle.

In 1949 Mr Macgregor and Colonel Shore, at the request of the National Trust, visited a number of sites along the Wall to view the differing methods of consolidation. At the time, at Birdoswald, Anderson was uncovering the east wall of the fort. MacGregor and Shore reported that the masons were re-laying the upper courses using 5:1 cement and pointing with 3:1 lime. Initially, a 25-yard section of Wall top of the east wall of the fort was left with a turf capping, but in 1952 Anderson was told to remove this and consolidate the top in cement. In August 1952, Anderson wrote to Mr Black, the Ministry's Superintendent of Works, regarding a visit to Birdoswald by Mr Wright, the Ministry architect:

> The Wall where the complete preservation work has been carried out is the east wall. Nothing of this wall was exposed when Mr. Wright visited the site. At the time he visited the west wall had been secured, also the south wall with the exception of a short section near the S-E corner, which he pointed

out he wanted treating the *dry way*. It was impossible to tear [tier?] the east wall in the dry manner, but … there is a section of this wall from the East gateway for approximately 25 yards where the turf was left on the Wall top. I will go to work on this at once, remove the turf and complete the wall top as core. This will save any trouble on this Wall from Mr. Wright. The south wall the two faces had been rebuilt with cement the top courses reset and remainder cement tamped, these lower courses were also seized behind with cement. Lime pointing has been carried out on the S wall south face. As I say this wall had been secured before Mr. Wright's visit.

West of Birdoswald, a length of Wall and a turret were exposed and consolidated between 1953–55. The turret, Birdoswald 49b, had been excavated in 1911 and then backfilled. Anderson recalled that

the north face was just a tumbled mess of thorns and trees and rubbish growing along the top. We excavated, cleaned it down and did the necessary preservation work on it. We had to bury one or two courses of masonry on its north side because they are down below the road level and it would have been dangerous to have left them exposed.

A phallic symbol was located on the upper course of the south face of the Wall 12 metres west of the turret.

The length of Wall from the fort eastwards to Harrow's Scar began to be opened up in March 1956 and immediately the masons found a phallic symbol built *in situ* on the south face of the Wall (Fig 2.51). Six centurial stones were then found *in situ* in the south face of the Wall, as was another phallic symbol. On the north face of the Wall east of the fort, Anderson photographed another section of Roman mortar spread, which had partly covered the outline of the individual blocks. Anderson fixed short pieces of non-rusting delta metal into the bottom courses of the Wall so as to help others locate the inscriptions and phallic symbols. However, very few of these tags remain. At least thirteen other centurial stones were recovered from the fallen facing stones of the Wall (see Appendix V). These eventually went to Tullie House Museum in Carlisle and the Museum of Antiquities in Newcastle. Some of the inscriptions had been found lying on the north side of the Wall. Anderson, who thought they had come from the north face of the Wall, mentioned this to Professor Richmond who replied, 'Well Charlie, we've not yet found any in position in the north face yet.' At a later date, Anderson was to find two centurial stones in the north face of the Wall, at Black Carts.

Sometime later the Wall was opened up from the Harrow's Scar end and work commenced in a westerly direction so that the two sections would eventually meet at the halfway point. When work commenced, the photographs show that the Wall was completely buried on the south face so that the top was level with the field. There had also been a stone wall with posts and rails alongside the Wall mound. The Ministry's official photographer, Mr Broadrim, took a number of photographs of the Wall between 1956 and 1958, showing the state of the Wall while work was being undertaken, as part of the official archive. Anderson noted that stones upturned during ploughing in the past had been thrown into the thorn hedge that had grown on top of the Wall. Up to ten courses of original Roman facing stones were found to have survived in an excellent state of preservation in this section: Anderson recalled that it was only necessary to reset the top course or two. He remarked on the thin string or bonding course of stonework that stretched across the width of the Wall. A large number of chamfered stones were found during the Ministry of Works operations along the length of Wall east of the fort, and these were stored in the south-west corner of Harrow's Scar milecastle (49). They were located again in 1991 (by Alan Whitworth), during the course of recording the fabric of the Wall, and are now housed at Birdoswald fort.

While working on this length of Wall in 1956, the Ministry masons came across the remains of a cist burial adjacent to the Wall face. Although burials of this nature in such a location are very unusual, no record of this discovery was ever noted or published, although a photograph of the remains exists in the English Heritage Photographic Archive (Crow and Jackson 1997, 65).

The cost of work at Harrow's Scar in April 1959, according to Anderson's records, was as follows: road widening of the track through the milecastle,

2.40. Birdoswald, east of fort, 1948. (Anderson)

2.41. Birdoswald, east gate, prior to uncovering, 1948. (Anderson)

2.42. Birdoswald, east gate being uncovered, 1948 (1). (Anderson)

2.43. Birdoswald, east gate being uncovered 1948 (2). (Anderson)

2.44. Birdoswald, east of fort, south face, looking east (1). (Anderson)

2.45. Birdoswald, east of fort, south face, looking east (2). (Anderson)

2.46. Birdoswald, east of fort, north face, Wall tumble. (Anderson)

2.47. Birdoswald, east of fort, south face, during consolidation. (Anderson)

2.48. Birdoswald, east of fort, being uncovered, showing height of surviving Wall face. (Anderson)

2.49. Birdoswald, east of fort, south face being uncovered. (Anderson)

2.50. Birdoswald, original Roman lime mortar. (Anderson)

2.51. Birdoswald, east of fort, south face, surviving Wall height, phallic symbol *in situ*. (Anderson)

2.52. Birdoswald, east of fort, prior to consolidation (1958–). (Anderson)

2.53. Birdoswald, north face of Wall, east of fort, during uncovering.
(Anderson)

£150 1s 5d; excavating the cutting back under the east wall of the milecastle,
£60 2s 3d; and the building of the retaining wall, £28 15s 0d.

The problem of the River Irthing undermining the steep slope of its west
bank had been recognised by Simpson and attempts were made to stabilise
the bank. The work involved tipping a large amount of soil over the cliff edge
onto a grille of timber and brushwood so as to stabilise the bank. In 1953
a proposal to inject subsoil grouting was turned down. Other suggestions
included revetting the scarp with a dry-stone wall construction and spraying
the area with tar. By 1955 the soil from the excavations at Birdoswald fort
was being tipped down the slope in an effort to give it a gentler gradient down
to the river bank.

When work commenced in 1956 on uncovering the Wall east of the fort,
the soil that was removed was also tipped over the cliff face at Harrow's Scar
to help alleviate the steep slope of the west bank of the river and so save the
milecastle from the possibility of sliding down the bank. Anderson says that
by January 1959 the masons had got the bank nicely built up and grassed
over but that it then collapsed into the Irthing, partly blocking the river and
bringing down trees in its wake. The Superintendent of Works judged that there
was the danger of a further collapse on the south-east side of the milecastle,
threatening to engulf the only access road to Underhaugh Farm, and was of
the opinion that saving of the milecastle was beyond human effort (EH file

AM 10350/01). Plans held by English Heritage include architects' drawings made in 1961 to try and solve the problem. During an inspection of the site in October 1967 following heavy rain, it was noted that approximately 100 tons of soil from the escarpment had fallen away and that the cliff face was within 3 feet 9 inches of the masonry.

Piper Sike Turret

Brought under guardianship in 1952, this turret was excavated in 1970 by Dorothy Charlesworth and members of the Cumberland and Westmorland Antiquarian and Archaeological Society prior to its consolidation by the Ministry of Works (Charlesworth 1973).

Lea Hill Turret

This was brought under guardianship at the same time as Piper Sike turret and was excavated in 1958 by Miss Charmian Phillips with the help of Charles Anderson and the Ministry of Works, who then consolidated the remains.

Pike Hill Signal Tower

Found, and partly destroyed, in 1870 when the road over it was lowered, the remains were examined in 1927, 1931 and 1932 (Birley 1961, 140). The signal tower was brought under guardianship in 1971; after which the stone wall on the south side of the road was taken down and replaced on a slightly different alignment and a public footpath created to allow visitors safe access from the turret to the signal tower. The author Hunter Davies passed by here on his *Walk along the Wall*. As he recounts:

> At Pike Hill ... I was pleasantly surprised to find signs of activity ... there were two Department landrovers parked outside a hut, a concrete mixer and some spades. One of the landrovers was very dirty and some joker had written in the dust 'Mr. Anderson, this car was late for work today'. (Davies 1976, 204)

Banks East Turret

The turret, discovered in 1927 and excavated in 1933, was, in 1934, the first section of curtain Wall in Cumbria to be placed under the guardianship of

2.54. Lea Hill Turret, 1958, prior to excavation. (Anderson)

2.55. Lea Hill Turret, 1958, during excavation. (Anderson)

the Ancient Monuments Department. The site and adjacent land were given by the landowners Lady Cecilia Roberts and Mrs W. Nicholson, after which the Ministry masons carried out consolidation of the fabric. Later, Anderson supervised repairs and first-aid work to the structure, adding new mortar where necessary.

Hare Hill

This short section of Wall came under guardianship in 1972. The masons exposed the lower courses at the base of the Wall on the north side, the rest of the upper fabric having been rebuilt by the Earl of Carlisle in the late nineteenth century. The south face of the Wall had been robbed in the medieval period, leaving only the core. A small section of Wall to the east of Hare Hill was inspected in May 1967 with a view to opening it up and consolidating the fabric. The cost of cleaning the site, excavation of the Wall, consolidation and pointing, together with making a path and putting up fencing, was estimated by the Superintendent of Works at £1,000. There is no evidence that this proposal was ever implemented.

Walton

This is the most westerly section of Wall that the Ministry masons uncovered. The 20-metre length of Wall came under guardianship in 1963 and authorisation was given by the Inspector of Ancient Monuments, Mr Gilyard-Beer, in February 1964, to commence with excavation and conservation work, after work had finished at Willowford West. The work was finally undertaken in the early 1970s under the direction of Dorothy Charlesworth (Snape 1996, 24). The masons exposed up to five courses of the porous red sandstone, but it was evident that the core and facing stones would not survive the inclement conditions. During the winter months it was covered with bales of straw given to Anderson by one of his farmer friends. The Wall was then uncovered in the spring for visitors to view. Of the bales of straw, Anderson says: 'I read somewhere once that it was a Ministry Inspector's idea. They hadn't the least idea why I did this.' In the early 1980s it was decided that the site should be permanently covered to preserve the deteriorating remains and consequently it was 'clamped' with soil and given a grass covering.

2.56. Walton, Wall of red sandstone (now reburied). (Anderson)

The Consolidation Method

The main aim of the Ancient Monuments Department was to conserve (not restore) the remains of buildings that came under its charge. In other words, the department's aim was that the Wall should not be reconstructed, but that it should be consolidated *as found*. No new stonework would be added and the minimal restoration that was carried out would be recognised as such.

Specifically, the masons on the Wall followed the methods of consolidation as recommended by the Ministry of Public Building and Works, as follows. After clearing the top of the Wall of any trees, accumulated soil and associated debris as far as the original Roman core, the Wall face was then exposed down to foundation level. It was often the case that the core of the Wall survived better than the pointing on the face, so that the task of building a modern mortar and stone capping to protect the core and to provide a water run-off was one of some skill. About 18 inches of the top of the core stones were then removed, cleaned and reset in a mortar bedding mix of Portland cement and sand in varying proportions of between 1:4 and 1:6. This was designed to shed water from the top of the Wall so as to prevent percolation of moisture into the remaining original Roman core.

In most cases it was necessary to remove several of the top courses of masonry facing stones as these were normally loose, out of line and required rebuilding. These building stones were numbered before removal from the Wall face to ensure that they were returned to their original position. The stones were washed clean and a bedding mix similar to that applied to the core was laid down and the stones reset in the Wall. It was envisaged that the consolidation work would have a life expectancy of twenty-five years.

The joints on the face of the Wall were then lime pointed. The hydraulic lime pointing mix contained a 'trowel full' of ordinary Portland cement to each bucket of lime. (For a record of the mortar mixes used on the Roman Wall, see Appendix III). Below the reset facing stones, the joints were raked out where necessary to a depth of 1–1½ inches, to remove all the dirt and loose mortar. The joints were then thoroughly cleaned with water before the new pointing was applied. After the lime mortar on the Wall face had partially set, it was sprayed with a water syringe which cleaned the sand and gravel in the lime mortar. It was desirable to avoid pointing during frosty weather but, where this was unavoidable, the work had to be protected by a covering of hessian sacking. It was also necessary to protect the new mortar during hot weather by dampening the covering.

Efforts were made to match the pointing with the nearest original mortar. By adjusting the grit content of the mix, and the use of judicial washing and brushing off, the masons hoped to produce a mortar that blended with the original work. A technical note issued in 1977 stated that the use of pigments for colouring core binder was not recommended and every effort should be made to achieve the original colour with selected aggregates or naturally coloured binders such as French hydraulic lime (DAMBH technical note, May 1977).

Anderson made it a habit to keep samples of the Roman lime mortar from each section of Wall: 'I used to keep it in little plastic bags in my office at Corbridge, but I suppose modern times have done away with all that sort of thing.' He remarked that finding sand must have been just as much a problem for the Romans who built the Wall as it was for the modern-day masons in their consolidation work. He noted that nearly every site had a slightly different texture.

> The sand would be coarse with a lot of gravel in it in some sites while others would have very fine soft sand, almost like river sand. I suppose the sand would be mixed with lime about 3 to 1. They would need an awful lot of sand.

Anderson noted that the texture of the original Roman lime mortar was studied for colour and the sand makeup. Samples were then mixed until they got the correct make-up – similar to the original – on each particular section.

In 1985 Mr J. A. Griffiths, Superintendent of Works for the North, based at Carlisle, made the following comments on the process, in the Roman Wall Mortar Mixes Report:

> [One] fact becomes patently obvious and that is that the bedding mix is invariably weaker than the pointing mix. The general philosophy that experience seems to have indicated is that thermal movement in large masses of mortared masonry is better able to be absorbed without fracturing when the hardening agent in the mortar is hydraulic lime and when the mix is calculated so that in its composition it does not compete with the stone for hardness. The practice of adding Ordinary Portland Cement to the hydraulic lime-based mortar was to provide a pointed surface more resistant to the rigours of summer and winter weather.
>
> With the demise of the last economically available source of hydraulic lime, technical officers of the Department of the Environment have been obliged to use Ordinary Portland Cement as a hardening agent together with the use of hydrated lime as a plasticising agent. Two problems have emanated from this; one, the difficulty of achieving the right colour of mix when dried out, and two, the considerable fracturing of the surface pointing caused by the imbalance in thermal expansion and contraction within the Wall due to the very hard pointing. Experimentation had proved that the mix of Ordinary Portland Cement-based mortar upon the Wall cannot be made any weaker as to do so renders the mortar very susceptible to frost action. From the practical standpoint it is evident that for the well being of the Monument as a whole an acceptable substitute for Ordinary Portland Cement as a hardening agent is urgently needed. (Johnson and Wright 1985, 11–12)

The Hadrian's Wall Mortar Project was begun in the 1980s to evaluate three mortar types: lime-based mortars, hydraulic lime-based mortars and cement-based mortars. This led to the development of a wider, full-scale research project, known as the Smeaton Project, which has been investigating the properties of lime-based mortars for several years.

Currently, English Heritage uses a hydrated lime and white cement mix that does not set as hard as the surrounding facing stones and also has an acceptable colour match to the original Roman mortar. Ordinary Portland Cement is no longer used by English Heritage in the consolidation work on Hadrian's Wall.

The Clayton Wall and the National Trust

John Clayton had employed workmen to uncover sections of Wall, to expose the surviving masonry, and to use the fallen facing stones from alongside the Wall to rebuild it to a uniform height. The reused material was laid, without mortar, in level courses on top of the original Roman remains and new core work was added from the fallen debris. A turf capping, taken from the surrounding grassland, was then added to the top of the Wall (Woodside and Crow 1999, 103). The rebuilt Wall also functioned as an effective field boundary along the top of the Crags. In some sections the rebuild was so carefully matched to the original work that it can be difficult to tell what is Roman work *in situ* and what is Clayton's work (Johnson 1989, 130). On close examination the original Roman work can generally be distinguished by areas of either surviving hard mortar between the stone joints or crumbling and perished mortar mixed with earth in which grows the lime-loving plant Maidenhair Spleenwort (*Asplenium trichomanes*).

The National Trust's method of preserving the fabric of the Wall within its estate generally followed John Clayton's principles, which were carried on into the early part of the twentieth century by F. G. Simpson.

However, Simpson was not uncritical of Clayton. He noticed that Clayton's opening of the Wall sometimes had detrimental effects. In particular, he noted the serious damage done by frost and rain on account of the wide joints in the Wall and the condition of the mortar.

> The latter, although extremely hard and well preserved at certain points, is for the most part soft, and in many places entirely decayed. As a result of exposure of the Wall from about the year 1848, the mortar was soon washed out of the joints, from the face inwards, causing the heavy, wedge-shaped stones to slide forward and downwards, thus affecting not only the top courses, but, frequently, the full height of the exposed face, which bulges and finally collapses, carrying away the whole front at that point. (Simpson 1976, 78)

Simpson considered that the only practical method of conservation was to re-bed some of the facing stones at vulnerable places, such as the corners of gateways, with a new mortar; but in the main, the work was to be dry-built. The facing stones were not re-dressed or altered but laid directly upon one another with the space behind the blocks being packed with small pieces of broken core.

Although the restoration work carried out by Clayton has been relatively successful, problems, unforeseen by Clayton, have occurred. The sections of 'Clayton Wall' that pass through the National Trust estate have suffered from frost, rain and stock damage as well as from the countless visitors walking on top of it over the decades. The erosion caused by visitors walking on the turf capping of the Wall increases the amount of water and ice entering the core and joints, thus causing further weakness and instability. The areas of 'Clayton Wall' that tend to collapse include areas of original Roman work, which survives to varying heights in the central sector. In these areas Harry Beamish, the National Trust archaeologist, reports that the organisation now uses a hydraulic lime and sand mortar to tail-bed the facing stones into the core to ensure that repair work on these vulnerable sections is kept to a minimum. The National Trust in recent years has been actively engaged in re-seeding and re-turfing the top of the relevant sections of 'Clayton Wall'. One of the aims of the Hadrian's Wall National Trail is to encourage walkers to use the path created alongside the Wall instead of walking along the top of the Wall. In this it has been very successful.

Consolidation and Controversy

Since 1933, when the first piece of the Roman frontier system was brought under guardianship, at Corbridge, there have been differing views as to the best method of preserving and protecting the Wall and its associated structures. The National Trust preferred the dry-stone walling and turf-capping method – 'the Clayton method' – as it saw the Wall as an aesthetically attractive feature in the landscape, while the Ministry of Works considered the use of a cement capping and lime pointing to be more appropriate to a national monument of such historical significance.

At Housesteads, when it became clear that the site would be placed under guardianship, the Trust argued that the turf capping on the fort walls and the rest of the Wall should be kept. Both parties solicited the views of archaeologists and professionals to support their preferred methods of preservation, and at times the relationship between the Trust and the Ministry became fraught. The amount of correspondence held by both the Trust and Ministry (now English Heritage) regarding methods of preservation is substantial.

As previously mentioned, on 10 October 1957 a meeting between the National Trust, the Ancient Monuments Board and the Ministry of Works was held at Lambeth Bridge House to try and establish a way of consolidating the Wall that would be satisfactory to all those concerned. Those attending included Lord Esher, Hon. Nicholas Ridley, Mr Romilly Fedden and Mr Acland of the National Trust, Sir Mortimer Wheeler, Mr Ralegh Radford and Professor Ian Richmond from the Ancient Monuments Board and Mr Baillie Reynolds, Mr Gilyard-Beer, Mr Rawson and Mr Lewis from the Ministry of Works. The Chairman, Sir Edward Muir, eventually ruled that the Ministry would continue to use the methods that they considered most effective on the sections for which they were responsible but in the central sector a compromise had to be achieved between the Trust and Ministry. He suggested that where the Trust had to undertake repairs in the sections they owned, original core-work and facing stones should be consolidated by the Ministry of Works methods, such pointing being undertaken as was necessary for adequate protection, the Wall being thereafter built with the recovered facing stones in the customary National Trust method with a turfed walk on top. In order to determine whether this proposal was practicable, there should be consultation between the Trust and Ministry so that a section of the Wall in National Trust ownership could be treated by the new method. It was agreed by all the parties that the compromise should be tried in an effort to reconcile the views of the National Trust and the Ministry on the treatment of the Wall. The report prepared by MacGregor and Shore for the National Trust in 1949 (National Trust files HW/EG 1948–50) concluded that the Roman core could not be left unprotected to disintegrate. Of the two methods of protection that had been used, the turf sod and the reconstructed core, the former would appear to be the less misleading and the more harmonious aesthetically while the latter might be more long-lasting. MacGregor and Shore concluded that perhaps the best solution would be to combine the advantages of both methods: by placing a protective course of stone in cement-mortar under the turf capping.

As early as 17 and 20 August 1947, letters had been printed in *The Times* regarding the methods of consolidation of the Wall. But serious public controversy was provoked by the publication in the *Observer* on 9 February 1958 of an article by the paper's archaeological correspondent, Mrs Jacquetta Hawkes, entitled 'Battle of Hadrian's Wall', in which she criticised the methods used by the Ministry of Works in exposing and consolidating the Wall. (A further article followed on 30 March.)

Mr Fedden, the secretary of Historic Buildings for the National Trust, replied in *The Times* on 16 February that, at the meeting between the Trust and Ministry, a programme of conservation for the important sections of the Wall owned by the National trust had been agreed with the Ministry. This provided for the retention of the turf capping on the Wall; but it was also agreed that the Trust would avail itself of the Ministry's expert advice in order to respect the archaeological interest of the Wall. This exchange of views raised the public's awareness of the conservation of the Wall, to the extent that the problem was debated in the House of Commons (*Hansard* 2 April 1958, 1323–56).

Mr Francis Noel-Baker MP (Swindon) quoted one of the allegations from the newspaper article:

It is reliably reported that on the section near Birdoswald four workmen are employed with only occasional supervision. They dismantle the Wall, nine feet at a time, stacking the square masonry and rubble filling and consolidating the foundations. The Roman mortar, which varied in colour from one age to the next and therefore shows repairs and alterations is destroyed without record. Far worse, the work emerging from the hands of these excellent workmen is not Hadrian's Wall at all. It is a copy - and one which has lost all the gifts of time.

He then quoted from the second article in the *Observer*:

The Minister stated that Roman masonry is never dismantled and rebuilt unless the stones are on the point of falling.

Dame Irene Ward MP (Tynemouth) said that both Mr Eric Birley and Mr John Gillam had replied to the newspaper article, paying tribute to the skill of the workmen engaged on the work. They also said that the Minister's replies (in defence of the consolidation work) were 'in complete accordance with their own personal observation over a long period of years'. Dame Irene Ward then stated her agreement with the Minister, the Right Honourable Mr Harmar Nicholls MP (Parliamentary Secretary to the Ministry of Works), that the views expressed in the original article were 'absolutely inaccurate and unfounded'.

The Minister then reiterated his own emphatic opinion, that of course there were two opinions on subjects like this:

the correct one and the incorrect. What is being done by my archaeological department ... is the correct line, while the line that takes the contrary view is the incorrect one. (*Hansard* 2 April 1958, 1327)

According to Mr Eric Fletcher MP (Islington, East):

There is the problem of whether or not the Department should preserve a monument in the precise form in which it is found, with all the accumulation of debris which has grown up around it since it was built, or whether there should not be a radical reconstruction, but a renovation in such a way to make the monument more easily intelligible to, and appreciated by, this generation ... [It] may well be that in the course of preservation something is done which necessarily or inevitably disturbs the original nature of the original fabric and the way in which the stones were placed. But I noticed that Mrs. Jacquetta Hawkes points out in her article in the *Observer* of 30th March: 'It would be unfair to say that historical evidence is being lost in this way, but indisputably it could be.' ... It is right that in this House we should take the opportunity of paying a tribute to the work that the Ancient Monuments Board has done in recent years in connection with the preservation of our ancient monuments.

Mr Nigel Nicholson MP (Bournemouth East and Christchurch), a lay member of the Ancients Monuments Board, pointed out that Mrs Hawkes was not only one of the most distinguished archaeologists of her day, but was able to marry scientific fact with a sense of landscape and culture. He continued:

> When the Ancient Monuments Board came to consider this matter of Hadrian's Wall, it went into it with the greatest care. It consulted not only with those archaeologists outside the Board who know most about the subject, but also consulted with the National Trust … and with private landowners. In each of these cases the Board came to the conclusion that there was no single treatment of the Wall which was suitable for every part of it.

He continued by saying that the Board had noted that a large part of the Wall is a reconstruction dating from the nineteenth century and that part of the Wall west of Housesteads (Clayton Wall) is more or less a fake in the sense that although the original stones were reused, they were pulled apart and replaced in an order, which did not necessarily correspond to the order in which they were originally found.

> The question arose, when new parts of the Wall were uncovered, should the Ministry treat them in exactly the same way as Mr. Clayton did, and which the National Trust followed, or should it evolve a method which would be archaeologically less defensible. The Ministry decided, and in this it had the complete backing of the Ancient Monuments Board for England, to preserve as much as possible of what it found, and to consolidate, render it waterproof, and, as far as possible, render it proof against the ravages of weather, sheep and trippers. If one has to choose between the National Trust method of preservation and the Ministry of Works method, the Ministry's method is certainly sounder from the purely archaeological point of view.

Interestingly, Mr Nicholson then suggested that the Ministry should conduct research into a new mortar to consolidate the remains.

Mr Harmar Nicholls MP (Parliamentary Secretary to the Ministry of Works) steered the debate back to the article in the *Observer*. He said there was no suggestion in the article that the general policy was wrong or deserving of criticism. The charge was that the implementation of the policy is at fault. He said it might be helpful to remind the House that the Ministry policy 'is to arrest the process of decay at a point which they have reached when we take over the responsibility. That is the basis of our policy and all the instructions on the work in hand flow from that.' The articles suggested that the use of careless workmen and the lack of general supervision risked destroying archaeological evidence. In answering this charge, Nicholls then went into some detail, describing the methods used to uncover the Wall:

> In sections of about twenty yards at a time a trained archaeologist and a Department architect accompany the superintendent of works on to the site and decide the character of the work to be undertaken and give detailed instructions to the charge-hand. In this case, the charge-hand [Charles Anderson] was a man of great experience, and in his private capacity is a member of the Society of Antiquaries of Newcastle. They pass detailed instructions through the superintendent to the charge-hand, who then instructs his leading hand and the workmen as to the detailed methods of handling and the removal of waste. He tells the workmen exactly how he wishes the work to be carried out. The method of handling and of moving it follows a drill which has been very carefully thought out and under which careful instruction is given until the men themselves have some experience of the work involved. The leading hand is on the spot the whole time the work is being carried out. When this has been done and the work has proceeded, the superintendent of works comes back at least every ten days to check over the type and quality of the work which has been carried out. Later the archaeologist and the architect again inspect to see how their instructions are being carried out. This procedure is meticulously carried out and even the author of the article, after having given this great message of carelessness and unskilled work, could merely say: 'It would be unfair to say that evidence is being lost'.

2.57. Jacquetta Hawkes and 'Cubby' Ackland. (National Trust)

Nicholls went on to point out that the Ministry of Works methods had been constantly under review and had been approved by the Ancient Monuments Board for England as well as established archaeologists such as Ian Richmond, Eric Birley and John Gillam. Other members of the Ancient Monuments Board, including Mr Ralegh Radford, Mr Gilyard-Beer and Mr Bruce-Mitford, had discussed the *Observer* articles and had expressed confidence in the methods used by the Ministry of Works.

It is now generally agreed that because the National Trust has had only limited resources and staff to carry out their responsibilities, certain sectors of the Wall have suffered over the years. Although there are still conflicting views on the most appropriate and effective way of conserving the different sectors of the Wall, the National Trust has accepted that the excavation and consolidation of those sectors of the Wall that pass through its estate should be carried out in accordance with the guidelines prescribed by English Heritage. For its part, English Heritage has acknowledged that as far as the 'Clayton Wall' is concerned it is acceptable for the monument to be maintained with a turf topping and that any repairs to the fabric blend in with the adjacent stonework. As well as ensuring there is a full and detailed record of the existing fabric of the Wall and any associated structures prior to any work being carried out, both English Heritage and the National Trust now employ professional archaeologists to oversee the work of consolidation. Prior to the mid-1970s, the only excavation carried out as part of the Ministry of Works consolidation programme was that carried out in July 1957 at Long Byre; hence Jacquetta Hawkes' concerns. However, it should certainly not be thought that these concerns reflect badly upon the work of Charles Anderson.

The Photographic Record

Charles Anderson's combined interest in photography and the uncovering of the Roman Wall meant that the photographic record he made of the work in progress has provided an invaluable archive that otherwise would not have existed. His photographs have provided a unique record of virtually all of the now exposed and consolidated sections of the Wall as they existed prior to the interventions by the Ministry of Works. It is only because Charles Anderson took it upon himself to compile a photographic record, and later an 8-mm colour cine film record, that present-day archaeologists are able to view the Wall as it was being uncovered and consolidated. No doubt, in recognising the obligation to make some form of permanent record of his work, Anderson was influenced by the various eminent archaeologists he met and with whom he liaised very closely. His dedication is witnessed in the number of inscriptions that were recovered from fallen material, photographed and recorded in various archaeological journals (Appendix V).

No archaeologist was assigned full-time to carry out recording of the exposed sections of Wall, but the Inspector of Ancient Monuments, based in London, made regular visits to view the work in progress and to give instructions on how to proceed. However, Anderson was generally given a free hand to carry out excavation and consolidation within the parameters of the inspector's instructions. The photographic record testifies to his careful observation and his determination that his men should maintain the highest standards. A set of albums of the Anderson prints is held by English Heritage in the Plans room in Swindon; and in 1997 the Royal Commission on the Historical Monuments of England made a full set of photographic prints, courtesy of the Vindolanda Trust, as part of the national archive.

A Walk along the Wall

In 1974 the Cumbrian author Hunter Davies published an account of his walk along the Wall from Wallsend to Bowness in the course of which he met Charles Anderson (Davies 1974, 214–23). Anderson, who was then sixty-five years of age and due to retire shortly, took Davies to Blackcarts and, as we have seen, explained to him the process by which the Wall was uncovered and consolidated. Anderson was always willing to talk to anyone with an interest in the Wall and to pass on any information that he thought might be of interest. In *A Walk Along The Wall* (1974), Davies repaid Anderson's generosity:

> Charles Anderson is one of the grand old men of the Wall, yet he never gets acknowledged in the reference books. All students of the Wall know about the work of Simpson and Richmond and Birley. Their contribution is in every book on Roman Britain and will never be forgotten as long as the Wall is studied. Yet Charles Anderson has given a lifetime to working on the Wall. More than anyone else, he can say that the Wall we see today is his. (Davies 1974, 216)

Anderson showed Davies some of the photograph albums of pictures he had taken over the years he had worked on the Wall and spoke with admiration of the work of Simpson, Richmond and Birley – and it is apparent that they had a mutual appreciation of the work being done by Anderson. At the end of their time together, Anderson presented Davies with three miniature altars, models of altars he had helped to conserve at Carrawburgh temple.

Cine Film

Aware of the importance of the operations that the Ministry was undertaking on the Wall, Anderson purchased an 8-mm cine camera to record in colour various aspects of his team's work. This he showed to any interested local organisations and groups. This invaluable archive appears to be the only cine film of work on the Roman Wall made by anyone from the Department of Ancient Monuments.

The uncovering and consolidation of the Wall at Willowford is extensively covered, and shows in detail the methods used by the Ministry of Works to conserve their ancient monuments: felling of the tress on the top of the Wall prior to exposing and cleaning the face and core; numbering, dismantling and cleaning the facing stones; re-bedding the facing stones and core with a cement and lime mortar; pointing the blocks with lime mortar; and washing off the mortar joints in the Wall face to produce a slightly roughened effect to leave the monument in its final consolidated state. The opening of the National Trust section of Wall east of Sycamore Gap towards Highshield Crags is shown but not the main consolidation programme that exposed a large amount of original Roman mortar.

The film includes the Durham Colleges Board Extra Mural Studies Summer School at Corbridge in August 1955, showing excavation on sites XI, XX and Temple III as well as a piece on cleaning and recording finds. Also recorded is the excavation of the hoard of Roman armour, weapons, tools and implements at Corbridge in 1964.

In 1963 Anderson filmed the discovery of the Roman auxiliary kilns in the playing fields of Irthing Valley School, now the William Howard School, at Brampton (Hogg 1965, 133–68). The latrines at Housesteads fort were filmed while workmen cleared the backfilled material from the earlier excavation prior to consolidation as well as scenes of the fort excavations (of the Commanding Officer's House and Hospital) directed by Dorothy Charlesworth in the late 1960s and early 1970s.

In recognition of the work that Anderson carried out over nearly four decades on the Wall (on behalf of the Ancient Monuments Department), with his work force of twenty-six masons and labourers, he was awarded the British Empire medal in 1968 and the Imperial Service medal in 1974. On 28 September 1969, the *Sunday Express* published an article on his work on the Wall in which Anderson was quoted as follows:

> There is a compulsion about the job in which you discover new things every day and it spreads to every man involved. I have chaps who have been with me since before the war and who wouldn't dream of leaving until they have retired.

The farmers along the Wall came to trust and respect Anderson as he understood their everyday life and would take the time to talk to them before dealing with issues like access to the site and the disposal of spoil from the excavations. He recognised that some farmers distrusted 'the men from the Ministry' and so he went out of his way to reassure them and to explain what he was trying to do to conserve the Wall. His invaluable ability to gain their respect made a huge difference to the smooth running of the consolidation of the Wall. On 21 March 1974 Charles Anderson finally retired as the Ministry of Works foreman on Hadrian's Wall; he passed away after a short illness on 3 November 1998, aged eighty-nine.

Epilogue

In 1987 the World Heritage Committee of UNESCO recognised the importance of the Roman Wall by confirming it as a World Heritage Site. There is no doubt that the invaluable contribution made by the Ministry of Works masons helped drive Hadrian's Wall towards its much-deserved international recognition. Indeed, all those mentioned in these pages have played their part. Their efforts have not only saved the Wall, but also built a bridge – a bridge from then to now.

2.58. Looking east to Housesteads. (Bill Brandt)

Appendix I

THE ANCIENT MONUMENTS ACT, 1931

Section 1. – (1) For the purpose of preserving the amenities of any ancient monument, the Commissioners may, subject to the provisions of this section, prepare and confirm a scheme (hereafter in this Act referred to as 'a preservation scheme') for any area comprising or adjacent to the site of the monument, being an area to which, in the opinion of the Commissioners, it is necessary or expedient for that purpose that the scheme should apply.

(2) Every preservation scheme shall define by reference to a map annexed thereto the area to which the scheme is applicable (hereafter in this Act referred to as 'the controlled area') and may provide for all or any of the following matters, that is to say:–

  (a) for prohibiting or restricting the construction, erection or execution of buildings, structures and other works above ground within the controlled area, or the alteration or extension of any such buildings, structures or works in such manner as materially to affect their external appearance;

  (b) for prescribing the position, height, size, design, materials, colour and screening, and otherwise regulating the external appearance, of buildings, structures and other works above ground within the controlled area;

  (c) for prohibiting or restricting the falling of trees, quarrying and excavations within the controlled area;

  (d) for otherwise restricting the user of land within the controlled area to such extent as may appear to the Commissioners to be expedient for the purpose of preserving the amenities of the monument;

  (e) for such other matters as appear to the Commissioners to be incidental to or consequential on the foregoing provisions of this section or to be necessary for giving effect to those provisions.

(3) The provisions of the First Schedule to this Act shall have effect with respect to the confirmation, variation and revocation of preservation schemes.

(4)   Nothing in any preservation scheme shall affect any building, structure or other work above ground or any alteration or extension thereof, if it was constructed, erected or executed before the date when notice of intention to confirm the scheme was published in the London Gazette under the First Schedule to this Act, and for the purpose of this provision a building, structure or other work and any alteration or extension thereof shall be deemed to have been constructed, erected or executed before that date –

(a) if its construction, erection or execution was begun before that date, or

(b) if and so far as its construction, erection or execution was necessary for the purpose of performing a contract made before that date.

(5)   Any persons whose property is injuriously affected by the coming into force of a preservation scheme shall be entitled to obtain compensation in respect thereof from the Commissioners, subject to the provisions of the Second Schedule to this Act.

(6)   If any person contravenes any provision of a preservation scheme for the time being in force, he shall be liable on summary conviction to a fine not exceeding twenty pounds for every day on which the contravention occurs or continues.

(7)   If, after any person has been convicted of a contravention or a preservation scheme by reason that any building, structure or other work is not in conformity with the scheme, the contravention continues after the expiration of such period as the court before whom he was convicted may determine, the Commissioners shall have power to do all such acts as, in their opinion, are necessary for removing so much of the building, structure or work as is not in conformity with the scheme, or for making it conform with the scheme, and any expenses incurred by the Commissioners in so doing shall be recoverable summarily as civil debt from the person convicted.

FIRST SCHEDULE

PROVISIONS AS TO CONFIRMATION, VARIATION AND REVOCATION OF PRESERVATION SCHEMES

1.   Before confirming a preservation scheme (hereafter in this Schedule referred to as a 'scheme'), the Commissioners shall cause to be published in the London Gazette, and in such other manner as they think best for informing persons affected, notice of their intention to confirm the scheme, of the place where copies thereof may be inspected, and of the

time (which shall not be less than three months) within which and the manner in which representations with respect to the scheme may be made, and shall cause such notice as aforesaid to be given to every local authority whose area comprises any part of the controlled area.

2. Any person affected by the scheme may, within the time appointed under the last foregoing paragraph for making representations, send to the Commissioners written objection to the scheme stating the specific grounds of objection and the specific modifications required.

3. The Commissioners, after considering any representations and objections duly made with respect to a scheme, and after consulting the Minister of Health and the Minister of Transport, may by order confirm the scheme either with or without modifications:
    Provided that –

  (a) where an objection has been duly made to the scheme by any person appearing to the Commissioners to be affected thereby and has not been withdrawn, the Commissioners, unless they consider the objection to be frivolous or have modified the scheme as required by the objection, shall, before confirming the scheme, direct a public inquiry to be held as hereinafter provided and consider the report of the persons who held the inquiry; and

  (b) a scheme as so confirmed shall not apply to any area to which it would not have applied if it had been confirmed without modification.

4. Any inquiry under this Schedule shall be held in accordance with rules made by the Commissioners for the purpose, and such rules may contain provisions as to the costs of the inquiry.

5. A scheme when so confirmed shall come into force on such date as may be specified in the order confirming it.

6. A scheme may be varied or revoked by a subsequent scheme, and the Commissioners may, after consulting the Minister of Health, by order revoke a scheme if they think in the circumstances that the scheme ought to be revoked.

7. As soon as possible after the making of an order under this Schedule confirming or revoking a scheme, the order shall be published in the London Gazette, and in such other manner as the Commissioners think best for informing persons affected, and a copy of the order shall be sent to every local authority whose area comprises any part of the controlled area.

8. In this Schedule the expression 'local authority' means, in England, the council of a county, county borough, county district or metropolitan borough or the Common Council of the City of London or, in Scotland, any county or town council.

SECOND SCHEDULE

PROVISIONS AS TO COMPENSATION

1. No person shall be entitled to compensation in respect of a preservation scheme unless within three months from the date on which the scheme comes into force, or within such further time as the Commissioners may in special circumstances allow, he makes a claim for the purpose in such manner as the Commissioners may by regulation prescribe.

2. A person shall not be entitled to compensation by reason of the fact that any act or thing done or caused to be done by him has been rendered abortive by a preservation scheme, if or so far as the act or thing was done after the date on which the Commissioners published in the London Gazette notice of their intention to confirm the scheme, or by reason of the fact that the performance of any contract made by him after than date is prohibited by the scheme.

3. Where any provision of a preservation scheme was, immediately before the scheme came into force, already in force by virtue of this or any other Act, no compensation shall be payable by reason of any property being injuriously affected by that provision of the preservation scheme if compensation has been paid, or could have been claimed, or was not payable, by reason of that property having been injuriously affected by the provision already in force.

4. Where any provision of a preservation scheme could, immediately before the scheme came into force, have been validly included, in a scheme, order, regulation or byelaw by virtue of any other Act, then –

    (a) if no compensation would have been payable by reason of the inclusion of that provision in that scheme, order, regulation or byelaw, no compensation shall be payable in respect of that provision of the preservation scheme; and

    (b) if compensation would have been so payable, the compensation payable in respect of that provision of the preservation scheme shall not be greater than the compensation which would have been so payable.

5. Any dispute as to whether any property is injuriously affected by a preservation scheme, or as to the amount of the sum which is to be paid as compensation in respect of such a scheme, shall be determined by arbitration under and in accordance with the Acquisition of Land (Assessment of Compensation) Act, 1919.

Appendix II

ANCIENT MONUMENTS ACT, 1931

ROMAN WALL AND VALLUM
PRESERVATION SCHEME
1938

Scheme for preserving the amenities of certain parts of the Ancient Monuments known as the Roman Wall & Vallum which run across Northumberland and comprise a stone wall with its ditch, camps, mile castles, turrets and subsidiary works and an earthwork or vallum running at various distances south of the stone wall.

1. Area of the Scheme.
The areas to which the scheme is applicable, hereinafter referred to as 'the controlled areas', are those which lie within the inner edge of the border coloured blue on the map annexed hereto.

2. Restrictions on User of Land and on building.
A. Within the controlled areas coloured yellow on the map: –
(1)   No new buildings, structures or other works may be constructed, erected or executed above ground except such as are to be occupied together with land which is used mainly or exclusively for agriculture, whether as arable, meadow, pasture ground or orchard or for the purposes of a plantation or a wood, or for the growth of saleable underwood, and is to be used for any of those purposes.
(2)   No new building, structure or work and no alteration or extension of any building, structure or work which might materially affect its external appearance shall be commenced until the site, elevation, design and materials of the proposed works have received the approval in writing of the Commissioner of Works.

B. Within the controlled areas coloured pink and edged red on the map: –
I. So long as those areas are held under the terms of any Lease or Agreement

for the purpose of the quarrying or working of any stone or minerals made before the date when notice was published in the London Gazette of the intention to confirm this scheme: –

(1)   No new buildings may be constructed, erected or executed above ground except such as are necessary for the purpose of any such Lease or Agreement.

(2)   No new building, structure or other work or alteration or extension of any existing building, structure or work may be carried to a height exceeding 70 feet from the natural ground level.

(3)   No building, structure or other work shall be constructed, erected or executed or materially changed in external appearance except in accordance with elevations and designs approved by the Commissioners of Works in writing.

II. So soon as these areas or any part thereof, cease to be held under any such Lease or Agreement, the same shall be subject to the restrictions on user of land and on building contained in the preceding paragraph A.

C. Within the whole of the controlled areas: –

(1)   Any person carrying on by himself, his agent or partner any manufacture, industry or occupation (other than agriculture, horticulture, forestry, farming, stock-keeping and the like industries) which it shall appear to the Commissioners of Works expedient to prohibit for the purposes of preserving the amenities of the monuments may be served by the Commissioners of Works with notice to discontinue such manufacture or industry within the controlled areas generally or within such portion or portions thereof as may be specified in the notice and such person shall within 3 months from the service of such notice discontinue such manufacture or industry accordingly. Provided however, that this prohibition shall not apply to manufacture, or industries which are already carried on in the controlled areas, at the place or places where they are so carried on at the date when notice was published in the London Gazette of the intention to confirm this Scheme.

(2)   No person may excavate for the purpose of obtaining any stone, minerals, sand or gravel or for any other purpose whatsoever or deposit slag heaps or refuse heaps of any description without the consent in writing of the Commissioner of Works who may grant their consent upon such conditions as to them may appear necessary to secure the preservation of the amenities of the Monuments.

Provided that stone or minerals may be quarried or worked in the areas coloured pink and edged red pursuant to and in accordance with (but not otherwise) the terms of any lease or agreement for the purpose of the quarrying or working of any stone or minerals made before the date when notice was published in the London Gazette of the intention to confirm this Scheme.

(3)   No person may construct any waterworks or reservoirs except on a site and in a manner approved of in writing by the Commissioners of Works, after consultation with the Minister of Health.

(4)   No works may be commenced for the widening or reconstruction of any existing road or for the construction of a new road without the written consent of the Commissioner of Works firsthand and obtained to the site and nature of the said works and to the manner of their execution; Provided that John Frederick Wake or any person deriving title under him and Sir Hugh Blackett and his successors and lessees in perpetuity may construct along the green line shown on the map annexed to this Scheme an approach road not exceeding fifteen feet in width from the Newcastle and Carlisle main road to his proposed quarry in the Melkridge area coloured pink and edged red. Such road shall be carried over the Vallum on a wooden trestle bridge which shall be removed by the said John Frederick Wake or his assignees at the termination of his present lease of the mineral rights if so required by the Commissioners of Works.

3. Control of Overhead Wires and Ropeways and Railways.

Within the controlled areas no overhead wires or ropeways or railways may be erected or constructed without the prior approval in writing of the Commissioners of Works both to the site and to the design of the proposed works, with the exception that John Frederick Wake or any person deriving title under him and Sir Hugh Blackett and his successors and lessees in perpetuity may construct a ropeway along the broken blue line shown on the map in the Melkridge area coloured pink and edged red provided that the standards of the said ropeway are so placed as not to interfere with the Vallum and the height of the standards does not exceed 50 feet above actual ground level; and with the exception that Sir Hugh Blackett and his successors and lessees in perpetuity may construct a separate aerial railway a light railway or any other reasonable means of access to and from his mineral area lying to the north of the northern boundary of the area coloured yellow in the map annexed, down to the London and North Eastern Railway at the Old Blackett Colliery Yard, Melkridge, adjoining the Three Horseshoes Inn, somewhere between the ropeway proposed to be constructed by John Frederick Wake under Section 3 of this Scheme and the western boundary of his royalty.

4. Restrictions on Advertisements and Petroleum Filling Stations.

Within the controlled areas: –

(1) No advertisement may be displayed or hoarding set up excepting advertisements or hoardings which relate solely to trade or business carried on or to an entertainment, meeting, auction, sale or letting to he held upon or in relation to the land upon which the said hoarding or advertisement is displayed. No board advertising properties for disposal or letting shall exceed six feet square in size, and on no property shall more than one such board be displayed unless such property exceeds ten acres in area in which case an additional board or boards may be displayed provided the approval in writing of the Commisioneers of Works is first obtained. No other advertisement or hoarding of any kind larger than six feet from the surface of the ground may be fixed to the outside wall of a building or to any other wall, fence or erection.

(2) No visible apparatus in connection with a petroleum filling station may be erected without the prior approval in writing of the Commissioners of Works alike to the site of the apparatus or station, the colour in which it is to be painted and its general elevation.

5. Application for Consent.

All applications under this Scheme for the consent or approval of the Commissioners of Works shall be made in writing and served upon them at His Majesty's Office of Works, Storey's Gate S.W.1., by being sent by post so addressed to them.

All applications, plans, sections and other documents delivered to H.M. Office of Works or to any official of the Commissioners of Works in pursuance of this Scheme shall on delivery become the property of the Commissioners of Works.

6. Powers of Entry.

The Commissioners of Works or any of their officers, servants or agents on production of the written authority of the Commissioners of Works shall after three days' notice to the occupier, if any, be admitted into or upon any property in the controlled areas at any time between the hours of 9 in the forenoon and 6 in the afternoon for the purpose of any inspection necessitated by the provisions of this Scheme or of ascertaining whether the provisions of the Scheme are being observed.

7. Notices required or authorized to be served under the Scheme.

Any notice required or authorized to be served under the Scheme upon the owner or occupier of any property affected by the Scheme may be served either by delivering it or leaving it at the usual or last known place of abode of the person on whom it is to be served or by sending it by post as a registered letter addressed to him at his last known place of abode or by fixing it on some conspicuous part of the property. Any notice may as the case requires be addressed to the 'owner' or 'occupier' of the property (describing it) without further name or description.

8. Interpretation

The Interpretation Act, 1889 (52 and 53 Vict. C.63) shall apply to the interpretation of this Scheme as it applies to an Act of Parliament.

9. Short Title and Deposit of Copies.

(a)   This scheme may be cited as the Roman Wall and Vallum Preservation Scheme 1938.

(b)   A sealed copy of this Scheme with map annexed shall be kept available for public inspection at all reasonable times at the Offices of the Commissioners of Works, Storey's Gate, S.W. 1 and other such copies shall be so kept at the Office of the Commissioners at 63, Westgate Road, Newcastle-upon-Tyne, at the Rural District Council Offices, Haltwhistle, Northumberland, and at the Rural District Council Offices, Priestpopple House, Hexham, Northumberland.

Appendix III

HADRIAN'S WALL MINISTRY OF WORKS MORTAR MIXES

The details below were obtained from a list provided by Mr R. Humbleby, Area Works Office, Carlisle Castle, c. 1985, and are based on his own recollection and on the memory of site staff concerned (Johnston and Wright 1985, 13). The hydraulic lime pointing mix contained a 'trowel full' of ordinary Portland cement to each bucket of lime. (OPC stands for Ordinary Portland Cement.)

MONUMENT	DATE	BEDDING MIX OPC; SAND	POINTING MIX OPC; LIME; SAND
Hare Hill	1973	1:5	½:1½:4
Banks Hill	1973	1:5	½:2:5
Lea Hill	1969	1:4	½:2:7
Piper Sike	1970	1:4	½:2:7
Birdoswald	1950–58	1:4	½:1:2 hydraulic lime (East Anglia)
Harrow's Scar	1959–60	1:4	½:1:2 hydraulic lime
Willowford & Bridge Abutment	1950	?	?
Milvain E + W	1970	1:4	?
Walltown Crags	1957–59	1:4	½:1:2 hydraulic lime
Cawfields West	1960–73	1:6	½:1:2 hydraulic lime
Cawfields East	1960–73	1:6	½:2:5 hydraulic lime
Winshields	?	?	?
Steel Rigg	Pre-1939	1:4 & 1:5	1:2:5 hydraulic lime
HOUSESTEADS			
Latrines	1963	1:4	½:1:2 hydraulic lime
Commander's House	1968	1:4	½:2:5 hydraulic lime
Barracks & Hospital	1972	1:5	1:2:5 hydraulic lime
Knag Burn Wall	1976, 1981	1:5	1:2:7 hydraulic lime

Sewingshields	1958	1:5	1:1:2 hydraulic lime
Sewingshields	1977	1:5	1:2:6 hydraulic lime
Carrawburgh	1955	1:4	1:1:2 hydraulic lime
Black Carts	1971	1:4	1:2:5 hydraulic lime
Chesters Fort	1956–62	1:5	1:1:2 hydraulic lime
Chesters Bridge	1982	1:4	1:2:5 hydraulic lime
Brunton Turret	1947	1:4	1:1:2 hydraulic lime
Planetrees	1948	1:4	1:1:2 hydraulic lime
Corbridge	Pre-1939	?	?
Heddon	Pre-1939	?	?
Denton East/West	Pre-1939	?	?
Benwell Temple	Pre-1939	?	?
Benwell Crossing	Pre-1939	?	?
Vindolanda	1972	1:4	½:2:5 hydraulic lime

Appendix IV

LIST OF ANDERSON PHOTOGRAPH ALBUMS
at the English Heritage Plans Room, Swindon

BENWELL VALLUM CROSSING, WEST DENTON, HEDDON ON THE
  WALL
BRUNTON AND PLANETREES
CHESTERS
BLACK CARTS
SEWINGSHIELDS
HOUSESTEADS VOL. 1. FORT WALLS AND GATES
HOUSESTEADS VOL. 2. INTERNAL BUILDINGS
HOUSESTEADS VOL. 3. HOSPITAL AND COMMANDANTS HOUSE
HOT BANK, WINSHIELD CRAGS, CASTLE NICK MILECASTLE 39
VINDOLANDA
CAWFIELDS VOL. 1
CAWFIELDS VOL. 2. MILECASTLE 42 AND AREA
GREAT CHESTERS, BINCHESTER, EBCHESTER, CORBRIDGE,
  CARRAWBURGH
WALLTOWN VOL. 1
WALLTOWN VOL. 2. ADDITIONAL PRINTS
GILSLAND, POLTROSS BURN AND MILVAIN
WILLOWFORD, HARROW'S SCAR VOL. 1
WILLOWFORD, HARROW'S SCAR VOL. 2. ADDITIONAL PRINTS
BIRDOSWALD
BIRDOSWALD TO BANKS
BANKS TO WALTON, HARE HILL, LANERCOST BRIDGE

Appendix V

Inscriptions found by Anderson during Consolidation

BLACK CARTS
   Britannia, vol. iii, no. 12. COH I >POM.RUFI PRIN PRIMI
   Britannia, vol. iv, no. 8. COH VI >.GELLI P ILIPPI
   Britannia, vol. iv, no. 9. COH.I NAS.BA
   Britannia, vol. v, no. 7. CRE > LABRI
SEWINGSHIELDS
   Britannia, vol. ii, no. 10. LEG VI VICTRIX PIA FID
   Britannia, vol. ii, no. 11. > GRAN
CHESTERS FORT
   JRS, vol. lii, no. 14. VAR.PATERNI P.VAL
HARROW`S SCAR TO BIRDOSWALD
   JRS, vol. xlvii, no. 16a. > TIIRTI
   JRS, vol. xlvii, no. 16b. > PP
   JRS, vol. xlvii, no. 16c. COH. III
   JRS, vol. xlviii, no. 10a. COH VI > FENI ALEX
   JRS, vol. xlviii, no. 10b. COH VI > EPPI CONST
   JRS, vol. xlviii, no. 10c. VIIS
   JRS, vol. xlviii, no. 10d. > PP
   JRS, vol. xlviii, no. 10e. > SECUND NI VERVLLI P XXX
   JRS, vol. xlviii, no. 10f. COH VIII > IVL PRIMI
   JRS, vol. xlviii, no. 10g. COH VIII > FLN BASI
   JRS, vol. xlviii, no. 10h. > VLP PAVLLI
   JRS, vol. xlix, no. 5a. > POMPEI AEMILIANI PXXX
   JRS, vol. xlix, no. 5b. > MARCI RVFI
   JRS, vol. xlix, no. 5c. > MARC RUF
   JRS, vol. xlix, no. 5d. < CARI SCIPIO
   JRS, vol. xlix, no. 5e. COH VII > ATILI NATALIS
HOUSESTEADS FORT
   JRS, vol. lvii, no. 17. AE VIT PRA EGA
SEWINGSHIELDS
   JRS, vol. xlix, no. 4a. C.X.> MV.MAXIMI
   JRS, vol. xlix, no. 4b. CANIONDICATUS

WALLTOWN
JRS, vol. l, no. 11a. LEG XX VV COH X > FL.NOR ICI
JRS, vol. l, no. 11b. COH VI CALEDO SECUNDI
JRS, vol. li, no. 11a. COH.I > LIBONIS
JRS, vol. li, no. 11b. VIII
JRS, vol. li, no. 11c. COH III > MAX TERN
JRS, vol. li, no. 11d. COH III > O
JRS, vol. li, no. 11e. > MARI DEXT
JRS, vol. li, no. 11f. > VAL VERI
JRS, vol. li, no. 11g. COH II > LAETIANI
WILLOWFORD AND MILVAIN
JRS, vol. lii, no. 19a. > VLPI VOLVSIINI
JRS, vol, lii, no. 19b. C CALEDON SECVNDI
JRS, vol, lii, no. 19c. COH.III > MAXIMI
JRS, vol, lii, no. 20. > P.P SERENI
JRS, vol. liii, no. 8a. COH III
JRS, vol. liii, no. 8b. > REGVLI
JRS, vol. xiv, no. 5a. COH II > OBC LIBO
JRS, vol. xiv, no. 5b. COH.I > VLS BINI
JRS, vol. xiv, no. 5c. COH III > SOCELLI
JRS, vol. lvii, no. 18. CO V AN
JRS, vol. lvii, no. 19. > IVLI.VALENI
JRS, vol. xlii, no. 6. COH VI > LOVSI SVAVIS
JRS, vol. xlii, no. 7. >. COCCEI REGULI
JRS, vol. xlii, no. 20. > P.P SERENI
JRS, vol. xliii, no. 8a. COH III
JRS, vol. xliii, no. 8b. > REGULI
JRS, vol. xliii, no. 8c. PETTA > DIDA
WILLOWFORD BRIDGE
JRS, vol. liii, no. 8c. PETTA > DIDA
JRS, vol. liv, no. 5a. COH II > OBC LIBO
JRS, vol. liv, no. 5b. COH.I > VAL SABINI
JRS, vol. liv, no. 5c. COH III > SOCELLI

PHALLIC SYMBOLS
Three phalli were found *in situ* in the Harrow's Scar-Birdoswald sector built
into the south face of the Wall.

CSIR 458. 193 metres west of milecastle 49.
CSIR 459. 375 metres west of milecastle 49.
UNRECORDED. 12 metres west of turret 49b.

Appendix VI

SECTORS OF HADRIAN'S WALL UNDER THE GUARDIANSHIP OF THE SECRETARY OF STATE

Note that unless recorded as a gift, these parts of the Wall and its associated works are in state guardianship but not ownership.

Site	Guardianship Date
CORBRIDGE ROMAN SITE (Gift)	15 May 1933
BENWELL VALLUM CROSSING (Gift)	4 June 1934
DENTON EAST AND WEST INCLUDING TURRET 7B	4 June 1934
BANKS EAST AND TURRET 52A (Gift)	14 August 1934
HEDDON-ON-THE-WALL (Gift)	9 May 1935
BENWELL TEMPLE (Gift)	18 January 1936
WINSHIELDS INCLUDING MILECASTLE 40	29 October 1937
POLTROSS BURN MILECASTLE 48	27 November 1938
WALLTOWN CRAGS INCLUDING TURRET 45A (Gift)	1 November 1939
VINDOLANDA STONE FORT & MILESTONE	5 November 1939
PLANETREES	30 June 1945
GILSLAND VICARAGE GARDEN	16 November 1945
CHESTERS BRIDGE EAST ABUTMENT	3 April 1946
SEWINGSHIELDS INCLUDING MILECASTLE 35 AND TURRETS 35A AND 35B	30 May 1946
WILLOWFORD	25 September 1946
MILVAIN AND TURRETS 48A, 48B	25 September 1946
BIRDOSWALD FORT CURTAIN WALL AND TURRET 49b	25 September 1946
HARROW'S SCAR MILECASTLE 49	25 September 1946
BRUNTON TURRET 26B	20 February 1947
BANKS HILL	26 July 1950
HOUSESTEADS FORT	12 October 1951
LEA HILL TURRET 51B	12 August 1952
PIPER SIKE TURRET 51A	12 August 1952
CARRAWBURGH MITHRAEUM AND MILECASTLE 31	30 July 1953

CHESTERS FORT   11 March 1954
CAWFIELDS CURTAIN WALL INCLUDING
MILECASTLE 42 AND TURRETS 41A, 41B   7 November 1960
WALTON-DOVECOTE BRIDGE (Gift)   19 January 1963
BLACKCARTS CURTAIN WALL
INCLUDING TURRET 29 A   18 May 1970
PIKE HILL SIGNAL TOWER   28 July 1971
HARE HILL   30 October 1972
CORBRIDGE-CORCHESTER HOUSE FIELD (Purchase)   7 July 1977

Bibliography

Anderson, Charles. *In the Footsteps of the Romans: Yesterday and Today.* Devizes Print. Limited family edition, undated.

Anderson, Charles. Transcripts of the tape-recorded commentary on the photographic record of the consolidation work done under his supervision by Charles Anderson, B.E.M., Foreman (retired). Transcribed by M. Savage. I. Stuart, Inspector of Ancient Monuments, 14 February 1980.

Bidwell, P. and Holbrook, N. *Hadrian's Wall Bridges: English Heritage Archaeological Report No. 9.* Historic Buildings and Monuments Commission for England, 1989.

Bidwell, P. and Watson, M. 'Excavations on Hadrian's Wall at Denton, Newcastle upon Tyne, 1986–89'. *AA*, 5th series, vol. xxiv, 1996.

Birley, E. Brewis, P. and Charlton, J. 'Report for 1933 of the North of England Excavation Committee'. *AA*, 4th series, vol. xi, 1934, 176–184.

Birley, Eric. *Research on Hadrian's Wall.* Kendal: Titus Wilson, 1961.

Birley, Eric. *Fifty One Ballades.* Hexham: privately printed, 1980.

Birley, Robin. *Vindolanda: A Roman Frontier Fort on Hadrian's Wall.* Stroud: Amberley, 2009.

Bishop, M. C. *Corstopitum An Edwardian Excavation.* London: English Heritage, 1994.

Bishop, M. C. and Dore, J. N. *Corbridge. Excavations of the Roman fort and town, 1947-80.* Archaeological Report No. 8. HBMCE, 1988.

Breeze, D. (ed.) *Handbook to the Roman Wall by J. Collingwood Bruce, 14th edition.* Newcastle: Society of Antiquaries of Newcastle, 2006.

Bruce, J. Collingwood. 'An exploratory turret of the Roman Wall'. *AA2*, vol. ix, 1883, 234–236.

Charlesworth, D. 'The Roman Wall at Cawfields'. *AA*, 4th series, vol. xli, 1963, 217–218.

Charlesworth, D. 'Recent work on Hadrian's Wall, Cawfields'. *AA*, 4th series, vol. xlvi, 1968, 69–74.

Charlesworth, D. 'A re-examination of two turrets on Hadrian's Wall'. *AA*, 5th series, vol. i, 1973a, 97–98.

Charlesworth, D. 'Hadrian's Wall, turret 51A (Piper Sike)'. *CW*, 2nd series, vol. lxiii, 1973b, 67–78.

Charlton, John. 'Saving the Wall: Quarries and Conservation'. *AA*, 5th series, vol. xxxiii, 2004, 5–8

Cherry, Gordon E. *Environmental Planning 1939–69. Vol. II National Parks and Recreation in the Countryside*. London: Her Majesty's Stationery Office, 1975.

Chesters Visitors' Books.

Collingwood, R. G. *Outlines of a Philosophy of Art*. Oxford: Clarendon Press, 1925.

Collingwood, R. G. *Guide to Hadrian's Wall*. Newcastle: Reid, 1st edn 1926, 2nd edn 1932, 3rd edn 1933.

Collingwood, R. G. and Taylor, M. V. 'Roman Britain in 1929'. *Journal of Roman Studies*, vol. xix, 1929, 180–218.

Collingwood, R. G. and Taylor, M. V. 'Roman Britain in 1930'. *Journal of Roman Studies*, vol. xxi, 1931, 215–230.

Collingwood, R. G. (ed.) *Handbook to the Roman Wall. 9th edition, by J. Collingwood Bruce*. Newcastle: Society of Antiquaries of Newcastle, 1933.

Collingwood, R. G. *An Autobiography*. Oxford: Clarendon Press, 1939.

Collingwood, R. G. *First Mate's Log*. Oxford: Oxford University Press, 1940.

Collingwood, R. G. and Wright, R. P. *The Roman Inscriptions in Britain, Volume I*. Oxford: Clarendon Press, 1965.

Coulston, J. C. and Phillips, E. J. *Corpus Of Sculpture Of The Roman World. Great Britain. Vol. 1, Fascicule 6. Hadrian's Wall West of the North Tyne, and Carlisle*. 1988.

Crow, J. and Jackson, M. *The Excavation of Hadrian's Wall at Sewingshields and the Discovery of a Long Cist Burial. AA*, 5th series, vol. xxv, 1977, 61–69.

Crow, J. G. 'A review of current research on the turrets and curtain of Hadrian's Wall'. *Britannia*, vol. xxii, 1991, 51–64.

Crow, James. *Housesteads: A Fort and Garrison on Hadrian's Wall*. Stroud: Tempus, rev. edn, 2004.

Cullingworth, J. B. *Environmental Planning 1939–69. Vol. I Reconstruction and Land Use Planning*. London: Her Majesty's Stationery Office, 1975.

Daniels, C. M. (ed.) *Handbook to the Roman Wall. 13th. edition, by J. Collingwood Bruce*. Newcastle: Society of Antiquaries of Newcastle, 1978.

Davies, Hunter. *A Walk along the Wall*. London: Weidenfeld & Nicolson, 1974.

Delaney, Paul. *Bill Brandt: A Life*. London: Jonathan Cape, 2004.

Earl, John. *Building Conservation Philosophy*. Whiteknights, Reading: College of Estate Management, 1997.

Fawcett, Jane (ed.) *The Future of the Past: Attitudes to Conservation, 1174–1974*. London: Thames and Hudson, 1976.

Gibson, J. P. and Simpson, F. G. 'The milecastle on the Wall of Hadrian at Poltross Burn'. *CW*, 2nd series, vol. xi, 1911, 390–461.

Gillam, J. P. 'Recent excavations at Birdoswald'. *CW*, 2nd series, vol. l, 1950, 63–68.

Gillam, J. P. Birdoswald: Unpublished Ms notes lodged with excavation archive at Tullie House Museum, 1952.

Griffiths, Clare V. J. *Labour and the Countryside: The Politics of Rural Britain, 1918–39*. Oxford: Oxford University Press, 2007.

Hansard, 2 April 1958.

Hassal, M. W. C. and Tomlin, R. S. O. 'Roman Britain in 1988'. *Britannia*, vol. xx, 1989, 6–11.

Hogg, R. 'Excavation of the Roman auxiliary tilery, Brampton'. *CW*, 2nd series, vol. lxv, 1965, 133–168.

Hutton, W. *The History of the Roman Wall*. London: J. Nichols & Son, 1802.

Joad, C. E. M. 'The Threat to the Great Roman Wall'. *Picture Post,* October 1943, 12–15.

Johnson, Stephen. *Hadrian's Wall (English Heritage)*. London: Batsford, 1989.

Johnston and Wright. *Roman Wall Mortar Mixes Report*. Unpublished report by Johnston and Wright, Architects, 15 Castle Sreet, Carlisle, 1985.

Jokilehto, Jukka. *A History of Architectural Conservation*. Oxford: Butterworth-Heinemann, 1999.

Lowenthal, David. *The Past is a Foreign Country*. Cambridge: Cambridge University Press, 1985.

Lubbock, John. 'On the Preservation of Our Ancient National Monuments' in *Addresses, Political and Educational*. London: Macmillan, 1879.

Mair, John and Delafons, John. 'The Policy Origins of Britain's National Parks: The Addison Committee 1929–31'. *Planning Perspectives*, 16:3, 2001, 293–310.

MacDonald, Sir George. 'Parker Brewis'. *AA*, 4th series, vol. xvii, 1940, 129–137.

Matless, David. *Landscape and Englishness*. London: Reaktion, 1998.

Miket, R. and Maxfield, V. 'The excavation of Turret 33b (Coesike)'. *AA*, 4th series, vol. l, 1972, 145.

Minute Book of the Housesteads Management Committee, 1930–49.

Morris, Richard. 'Breathing the Future: The Antiquaries and Conservation of the Landscape, 1850–1950' in *Visions of Antiquity* (ed. Susan Pearce). London: Society of Antiquaries, 2007.

N.R.O. (Northumberland Record Office). Melkridge (H) CLAs 148 (Clayton Estate Sale Catalogue).

N.R.O. SANT/ADM/5/1/1 (Peers' letter discussing the future conservation of the Wall, 21/2/28).

Parker, John. *Haltwhistle and Beyond*. Newcastle: TUPS Books.

Parker, John. *Cawfields Quarry and Railway*. Newcastle: TUPS Books.

Piggott, Stuart. *William Stukeley: An Eighteenth Century Antiquary*. London: Thames & Hudson, rev. edn, 1985.

P.R.O. WORKS 30/60/691 (Hadrian's Wall – the Oxford and Cambridge campaigns).

P.R.O. WORKS 14/1257 (includes press cuttings relating to Lansbury's visit to the Wall).

P.R.O. WORKS 14/1259 (Hadrian's Wall).

P.R.O. WORKS 14/1260 (Hadrian's Wall).

P.R.O. WORKS 14/1124 (Hadrian's Wall).

P.R.O. WORKS 14/1287 (Hadrian's Wall).

P.R.O. WORKS 14/488 (Stonehenge).

P.R.O. WORKS 16/853 (National Parks).

P.R.O. WORKS 16/855 (National Parks).

P.R.O. WORKS 16/856 (National Parks).

'Report of the Council of the Society for the Promotion of Roman Studies for the year 1930'. *Journal of Roman Studies*, vol. xx, 1930, 124–128.

Richmond, I. A. 'A Roman wrist-purse from Birdoswald'. *CW*, 2nd series, vol. l, 1951, 69.

Richmond, I. A. and Gillam, J. P. 'The temple of Mithras at Carrawburgh'. *AA*, 4th series, vol. xxix, 1951, 1–92.

Richmond, I. A. 'Excavations at Milecastle 49 (Harrow's Scar), 1953'. *CW*, 2nd series, vol. lvi, 1956, 18–27.

Richmond, John. 'Classics and Intelligence: Part I'. *Classics Ireland*, vol. viii, 2001.

Richmond, John. 'Classics and Intelligence: Part II'. *Classics Ireland*, vol. ix, 2002.

Rivet, A. L. F. 'Rudyard Kipling's Roman Britain'. *The Kipling Journal*, June 1978.

Robertson, Mairi. 'Conservation Practice and Policy, 1882–1945'. Master's Thesis (kept at Rewley House, Oxford), 2000.

Rushworth, A. and Barker, L. *Hadrian's Wall at Winshield Crags, Cawfield Crags and Walltown Crags*. English Heritage Historic Properties (North), 1997.

Salway, P. 'Excavations at Longbyre (Haltwhistle Parish)'. *AA*, 4th series, vol. xxxvii, 1959, 211–213.

Shaw, R. C. 'Excavations at Willowford'. *CW*, 2nd series, vol. xxvi, 1926, 429–506.

Shepherd, John. *George Lansbury: At the Heart of Old Labour*. Oxford: Clarendon Press, 2002.

Simpson, F. G. 'Excavations on Hadrian's Wall in the Gilsland-Birdoswald-Pike Hill sector, 1927'. *CW*, 2nd series, vol. xxviii, 1928, 377–388.

Simpson, F. G. *Watermills and Military Works on Hadrian's Wall* (ed. Grace Simpson). Kendal: Titus Wilson & Son, 1976.

Sheail, John. *Rural Conservation in Inter-War Britain*. Oxford: Clarendon Press, 1981.

Smiles, Sam. 'Equivalents for the Megaliths: Prehistory and English Culture, 1920–50' in *The Geographies of Englishness: Landscape and the National Past 1880–1940* (eds. David Peters Corbetts, Ysanne Holt and Fiona Russell). London: Yale University Press, 2002.

Snape, M. *Hadrian's Wall from Piper Sike Turret (51a) to Dovecote Bridge (near 55b)*. English Heritage Historic Properties (North), 1996.

Taylor, A. J. P. *English History, 1914–1945*. Oxford: Clarendon Press, 1965.

Taylor, Harvey. *A Claim on the Countryside: A History of the British Outdoor Movement*. Keele University Press, 1997.

Taylor, M. V. and Collingwood, R. G. 'Roman Britain in 1929'. *Journal of Roman Studies*, vol. xix, 1929.

Whitworth, A. M. 'Recording the Roman Wall'. *AA*, 5th series, vol. xxii, 1994, 67–77.

Whitworth, A. M. *Hadrian's Wall: Some Aspects of its Post-Roman Influence on the Landscape*. British Archaeological Reports, No. 296, 2000.

Whitworth, A. M. 'A 19th-century condition survey of Hadrian's Wall: The James Irwin Coates Archive, 1877–1896' in *Hadrian's Wall Archaeological Research by English Heritage, 1976–2000* (ed. T. Wilmott) English Heritage, 2009.

Woodfield, C. C. 'Six turrets on Hadrian's Wall'. *AA*, 4th series, vol. xxxxiii, 1965, 87–200.

Woodside, R. *The National Trust Archaeological Survey. Hadrian's Wall Estate. Vol. I. 1995*.

Woodside, Robert and Crow, James. *Hadrian's Wall: An Historic Landscape*. The National Trust, 1999.

Wright, R. P. 'Roman Britain in 1943'. *Journal of Roman Studies*, vol. xxxiv, 1944, 76–91.

Wright, R. P. 'Roman Britain in 1951'. *Journal of Roman Studies*, vol. xlii, 1952, 86–109.

Wright, R. P. 'Roman Britain in 1960'. *Journal of Roman Studies*, vol. li, 1961, 194, 11.

Index